Faith on the Edge

Edge

DARING
to Follow
Jesus

D0043624

Paul Tokunaga (editor), Kevin Blue,
Amy Brooke, Robbie Castleman,
Bobby Gross & Jon Tran

DATE DUE

InterVarsity Press
Downers Grove, Illinois

InterVarsity Press
P.O. Box 1400, Downers Grove, IL 60515
World Wide Web: www.ivpress.com
E-mail: mail@ivpress.com

InterVarsity Press® *is the book-publishing division of InterVarsity Christian Fellowship/USA*®, *a student movement active on campus at hundreds of universities, colleges and schools of nursing in the United States of America, and a member movement of the International Fellowship of Evangelical Students. For information about local and regional activities, write Public Relations Dept., InterVarsity Christian Fellowship/USA, 6400 Schroeder Rd., P.O. Box 7895, Madison, WI 53707-7895.*

All Scripture quotations, unless otherwise indicated, are taken from the New Revised Standard Version of the Bible, *copyright 1989 by the Division of Christian Education of the National Council of the Churches of Christ in the USA. Used by permission. All rights reserved..*

Cover illustration: David Zentner

ISBN 0-8308-2212-7

Printed in the United States of America ∞

Library of Congress Cataloging-in-Publication Data

Faith on the edge : daring to follow Jesus / Paul Tokunaga (editor) ;
  Kevin Blue . . . [et al.].
      p.   cm.
  Includes bibliographical references.
  ISBN 0-8308-2212-7 (pbk. : alk. paper)
    1. Christian life.   I. Tokunaga, Paul.   II. Blue, Kevin.
  BV4501.2.F286   1999
  248.4—dc21   99-43126
                                                                                  CIP

---

15   14   13   12   11   10 9 8 7 6 5 4 3 2 1

10 09 08 07 06 05 04 03 02 01 00 99

*If you are not living on the edge,
you're taking up too much space.*
LOU WHITAKER

*As individual writers, we dedicate this book
to those who cared enough to put
their "faith on the edge" for us:*

From Kevin to Brenda Salter-McNeil, and Mel and Tricia Campbell
From Amy to Sandy Beelen and Crystal Hiser
From Robbie to Diane and Randy McGirr
*From Bobby to InterVarsity's New York/New Jersey
     leadership team*
From Paul to Gary Fischer
From Jon to Thomas Christopher Allen

*And as a writing team, we dedicate this book to David Scott,
long-time and legendary InterVarsity student,
local supporter extraordinaire and member of the board
of trustees. More than his generosity in "giving"
us his home in Atlanta, where we twice met to dream/write/critique
this book, David's life as a disciple of Jesus
models what we have tried to describe in* Faith on the Edge.

Part 3: Disturbing the World

Foreword

The first time I read the manuscript of *Faith on the Edge*, I was in Seoul, Korea, attending the quadrennial World Assembly of the International Fellowship of Evangelical Students. Representatives from 134 countries were present. They were of every color of the human rainbow and from virtually every time zone around the world. It was a summer marked by news of ethnic and civil wars around the world. Yet at the World Assembly there were believers from Serbia *and* Albania, from Ethiopia *and* Eritrea, from India *and* Pakistan, from Israel *and* the Palestinian Territories. The one thing that all these people have in common is Jesus and the wisdom which is growing in them as Jesus' disciples.

As I read *Faith on the Edge* against this backdrop, several thoughts occurred to me.

First, I thought about how much "the fear of the Lord" or following Jesus really does change people. It is truly the "beginning of wisdom" (Proverbs 9:10; 15:33). Every life has its challenges. No matter where we grow up, we are affected by the brokenness of sin and are in need of radical transformation if we are ever to look like Jesus. Being "born again" is only the first step of a long journey. But no one can truly follow Jesus over time without being significantly changed from the inside out.

Faith on the Edge is a book about this kind of transformation. It is a book about the kind of wisdom that leads to changed lives.

Second, we need the broad and varied perspectives of people with different backgrounds and experiences to catch even a flicker of the full glory of life in Christ. One of the wonders of *Faith on the Edge* is that it is written by six people with widely differing experiences—in ethnicity, in geography, in age, in gender, in denominational involvement and so forth. Like my experience among believers from many countries, there is a greater awareness of the full image of God when God's character is displayed through a wider breadth of the community of faith.

Third, I thought about how complex and difficult following Jesus can be. Reflecting on my own struggles to be the person God wants me to be and to do the things that God wants me to do, I recognized again how much we need each other's help and encouragement. We need fellow believers to point us in the right direction and to encourage us along the way. We need their perspective and the wisdom that God has given them.

Faith on the Edge represents years of accumulated wisdom from those who have walked faithfully themselves and diligently with others. In the complexities of life it is refreshing to know that we are not alone and that God does have a plan which will lead us toward wholeness.

Fourth, I realized again that discipleship is a journey. I would prefer that transformation come quickly and painlessly, but that is not the way of it. As I listened to representatives at the World Assembly talk about their long journeys toward forgiveness and reconciling with others, or toward deep healing of the brokenness resulting from years of accumulated sin or abuse, I paused in gratitude for God's gift of the Holy Spirit to lead the process and the gift of the family of faith to hold us along the way. *Faith on the Edge* is a book that acknowledges the journey of discipleship and provides both the sustenance and guidance that we need to get on with it.

Here are chapters that I will personally reflect on again and again. I continue to come back to many of the same basic issues in my own walk. Like Peter, Jesus' disciple, I continually need to be reminded by the Master: "Follow me!" Peter heard these words from Jesus when he was first called (Mark 1:17). He heard them again when he thought that he knew better than Jesus did how to move into the future (Mark 8:33-35). And he heard them after he had denied his Lord and was in need of restoration and encouragement (John 21:18-11). Discipleship is about following Jesus. Only in following Jesus will we ever grow in true wisdom.

Stephen A. Hayner

part one

Rooted in Christ

"He who has a why to live for
can bear almost any how."
FRIEDRICH NIETZSCHE

"The passion of Christianity
is that I deliberately sign away my rights
and become a bond slave of Jesus Christ.
Until I do that, I do not begin to be a saint."
OSWALD CHAMBERS

"Yet whatever gains I had, these I have come to
regard as loss because of Christ. More than that,
I regard everything as loss because of the surpassing
value of knowing Christ Jesus my Lord. For his sake
I have suffered the loss of all things, and I regard
them as rubbish, in order that I might gain Christ
and be found in him, not having a righteousness of my
own that comes from the law, but one that comes through
faith in Christ, the righteousness from God based on faith.
I want to know Christ and the power of his resurrection
and the sharing of his sufferings by
becoming like him in his death, if somehow
I may attain the resurrection from the dead."
THE APOSTLE PAUL TO THE CHURCH IN PHILIPPI

one

What Is a Disciple?

Paul Tokunaga

S AM AND I WERE IN THE NOSEBLEED SECTION, 408 IN THE *UPPER* upper deck. Binoculars were a no-brainer. Without them, all on the track were color-coordinated ants. But no matter, my son and I were at Olympic Stadium, *at the 1996 Olympic Games, in our town, Atlanta.*

Juli Henner was not favored to win the 1,500 meters. Heck, we didn't even know who Juli was before that day. But she was an American. There was a little bit of us in Juli as she ran her heart out. As she leaned into the last turn on the oval, she was several lengths behind the front-runner. We risked further nosebleed damage by jumping to our feet and screaming until it hurt.

"Go, Juli, go! You can catch her! Push it, woman! Don't quit! You're gaining, you're gaining! Only a hundred more yards! Push it!"

Faith on the Edge
Having "faith on the edge" is something like that race.

> Therefore, since we are surrounded by so great a cloud of witnesses, let us
> also lay aside every weight and the sin that clings so closely, and let us run
> with perseverance the race that is before us, looking to Jesus the pioneer and
> perfecter of our faith, who for the sake of the joy that was set before him
> endured the cross, disregarding its shame, and has taken his seat at the right
> hand of the throne of God. (Hebrews 12:1-2)

Besides possibly being the longest sentence in the Bible, these two
verses spell out: *you are not alone.* There's a great cloud of witnesses.
There's Abel. There's Enoch and Noah. Abraham lets out a raucous cheer
for you. Jacob high-fives son Joseph. Watching is too much for Moses. He
one-arms himself over the barricade separating athletes from the masses.
You're gasping for oxygen. "I . . . don't . . . know . . . if . . . I . . . can . . . finish," your body pleads to your brain.

Moses must have read your mind. He matches you step for step on the
outside of the track. "We've run this race before! [Huff] Look at Rahab up
there—she made it! We know you can make it! We believe in you! Don't
quit! [Puff] Don't stop! You *can* do it!"

The life of a disciple of Jesus is no spring picnic. To follow Jesus does
not mean we modify our lifestyles a little here, a little there, allowing us to
look at our inner mirror and say, *Not too bad—for me.* It's more like the
analogy C. S. Lewis gives us in *Mere Christianity:*

> Imagine yourself as a living house. God comes in to rebuild that house. At
> first, perhaps, you can understand what he is doing. He is getting the drains
> right and stopping the leaks in the roof and so on: you knew that those jobs
> needed doing and so you are not surprised.
>
> But presently he starts knocking the house about in a way that hurts
> abominably and does not seem to make sense. What on earth is he up to? The
> explanation is that he is building quite a different house from the one you
> thought of—throwing out a new wing here, putting on an extra floor there,
> running up towers, making courtyards.
>
> You thought you were going to be made into a decent little cottage: but he
> is building up a palace. He intends to come and live in it himself.

The author of Hebrews writes with drop-dead candor about the life of a
disciple of Jesus. It is not easy. It is not always joyful. Some have been tor-

tured, others mocked and flogged, still others chained and imprisoned. And if you still haven't gotten the picture: "They were stoned to death, they were sawn in two, they were killed by the sword" (Hebrews 11:37). This is no social club we are joining.

What the life of faith is, on the other hand, is an incredible journey into the unknown. Armed with not much else besides the Father, the Son and the Holy Spirit, we are asked to fight powers and principalities. We are asked to be his ambassadors to those the world deems valuable—the powerful, the famous, the beautiful—as well as those deemed worthless—the weak, the expendable, the outcasts—and everyone in between.

Following Jesus means living by *faith on the edge*. This is the narrow gate Jesus talks about. Few dare to enter through it. In these pages six writers have selected two dozen areas where faith must be exercised if we are to be identified with Jesus by the watching world. Are they the only areas where we must exercise faith? No. But it is a good start.

God Was There

Before God was a thought in my little head, Jesus was laying the foundation for his palace.

I was eighteen months old. Our family of four was driving to a picnic, enjoying the present moment and looking forward to the years before us. If Norman Rockwell ever needed an Asian American family to pose for a *Saturday Evening Post* cover, we were it.

A drunk driver suddenly crossed the dotted line on the country road and hit us head-on, crushing our car. Mom flew out the windshield. She died instantly. Dad was pronounced dead but somehow lived. His face was like a puzzle with its pieces out of place. My older sister (almost five) and I were badly injured but survived—at least physically.

Dad remarried eighteen months later. He and my new stepmom worked hard to forge a new family, but it didn't come easily. My older sister and I felt that Mom #2 favored her own "full" children over her two older stepchildren. When I became filled with rage toward her (which, in retrospect, had less to do with her and more to do with losing my birthmom), I would get back at her by going out to our back patio and slamming my glasses on the concrete floor, shattering them far beyond repair. This satisfied my need for retaliation until Mom said, after I had shattered my third pair, "The next one's on you." I was a confused, despairing teenager, dying to be loved by someone in ways that connected with my heart and soul.

Discipleship 101

Somehow I ended up at a Young Life conference during my senior year of high school. There, I heard about an amazing person that I was clueless about. It was Jesus.

At the conference I heard this story: There was a woman caught in an act of adultery. She was thrown at Jesus' feet by religious leaders. They challenged him to deal with her rightly. He responded, "Let anyone among you who is without sin be the first to throw a stone at her." When they all sheepishly tip-toed away, Jesus asked the woman, "Woman, where are they? Has no one condemned you? . . . Neither do I condemn you. Go your way, and from now on do not sin again" (John 8:1-11). Unbelievable!

Being just seventeen, adultery was not my problem, but I knew clearly that I was a sinner in need of redemption of some sort. Could it possibly be true? A few weeks later I chose to be a disciple of Jesus. I knew little of Christianity. I had been a follower of the Buddha, as had generations in both my dad's and stepmom's families. I hardly knew to whom or to what I was committing myself.

It was several years later that I read some of the fine print. Jesus said:

If any want to become my followers, let them deny themselves and take up their cross and follow me. For those who want to save their life will lose it, and those who lose their life for my sake, and for the sake of the gospel, will save it. For what will it profit them to gain the whole world and forfeit their life? Indeed, what can they give in return for their life? (Mark 8:34-37)

Gulp. I had not bargained for becoming that palace in which Jesus would make himself at home. I was just looking for a wing here, a tower there.

Trying to make sense of Jesus' world, my development as a new disciple of Christ's was a real struggle. In my first few months as a "disciple"

☐ I went to prayer meetings loaded on marijuana.

☐ I found it hard to not pepper my prayers with "salty" language from my pagan past.

☐ After a Bible study on Matthew 14:28-33, I was so inspired by Peter's walk on water, that I tried it for myself in a nearby swimming pool. When the water wouldn't hold me (ruining a great pair of boots), I somehow was able to keep trusting Jesus. I rationalized, "Maybe it was just an off day for him."

☐ I told my parents as we stood at the family altar of our Buddhist temple on New Year's Day that I was now a follower of Jesus (one week old to the day), and we Christians did not do these kinds of pagan things, thank you.

After a few months as a Christian I began wondering, *Is this real? Is Jesus really inside of me? Did I just suffer a momentary relapse from Buddhism?* I noticed a few changes for the better, but not many.

Discipleship 201

I was a six-month-old follower of Jesus when I picked up the phone and gave Mom a call. I had moved out the day after high-school graduation and was working as a houseboy/cook for a household of bachelors, widowers and divorcees about eight miles from home. There was just one problem in taking this job: I didn't know how to cook. But I had managed to cook dinner for these men for about three weeks, and my confidence was growing.

"Mom, this is Paul. Hey, for your birthday next Thursday, why don't you invite Uncle Don and Auntie Joan over for dinner. I'm going to cook you a Chinese dinner for your birthday."

Her long pause finally ended with an uncertain "Sure . . ."

I hung up the phone and then panicked. I had never cooked Chinese food before! Mom was the best Chinese cook (even for a Japanese person) around! *What have I done? What if I kill them!*

Thursday came, and there I was in my little VW Karmann Ghia, balancing steaming containers of sweet and sour this and stir-fry that on the floorboards. *Oh, God, please let them live!* The moment of truth came; dinner was served. They all looked curiously at my offerings. Mom took a bite. *Oh, God . . . !* The look on her face was one I can't recall seeing before that night. There were no words but the look said this: "Something is going on in Paul. He would never have done this last year."

As I drove away, *wham!* it hit me. God *is* real. God *is* in me—I was starting to love Mom. I knew that love like that had only one source: the God of love. God could have parted the Red Sea or shown up in a burning bush and it would not have been a greater miracle than the one I was now experiencing. *I loved Mom and she knew it!*

A Richer Person, A Better Son

What is a disciple? According to the *New Bible Dictionary* a disciple is, basically, the pupil of a teacher. A Christian disciple, logically, is a pupil of Jesus. In the Gospels the term is applied "to all who responded to his message."

Did you catch the punch line? Disciples are not those who go to every Bible study, never lose their temper and always have a positive mental attitude. Disciples aren't those who remain unstained from the world because they never venture into it. No, disciples are those who *hear* Jesus' message and *obey* it.

We live right smack in the world. We rub shoulders with sinners. We keep both ears and eyes wide open for ways to use our hands, feet and hearts to show them we truly love them. We even create those opportunities from time to time, like cooking a quasi-Chinese meal.

In the years that followed that memorable meal I cooked for Mom, I have remained a disciple of Jesus. In my own awkward way I've said to him, "My life belongs to you. I will deny myself, take up my cross and follow you. I am willing to lose my life for the sake of the gospel. Just show me how."

Last December marked for me thirty years of being in God's family. When I look in the mirror, I know it's the same body, basically speaking, that I had thirty years ago. Paul Tokunaga then, still Paul Tokunaga now. My friends from my senior year in high school would easily recognize me at our next high-school reunion (At the ten-year reunion, they informally dubbed me "the one who had changed the least".) But most of the comparisons end there. The promise of being a new creation—"everything old has passed away; see, everything has become new!"—is happening in my life. Am I perfect? Hardly (ask my wife of twenty-two years). Am I a new creation? Absolutely (again, ask my wife).

A promise from God that has sustained me these thirty years is found in Jesus' words to his disciples: "Everyone who has left houses or brothers or sisters or father or mother or children or fields, for my name's sake, will receive a hundredfold, and will inherit eternal life" (Matthew 19:29).

As Buddhists, my parents have not celebrated my decision to follow Jesus. However, they have respected and honored that choice in a remarkably loving way. I am so grateful for them. But when I chose Jesus, I chose a wholly different path from theirs. It wasn't and isn't easy. The Lord has celebrated and honored that choice at least a hundredfold. I am a richer person and a better son because Jesus *is building a palace in me.* My life's goal is to keep saying with the apostle Paul:

> I want to know Christ and the power of his resurrection and the sharing of his sufferings by becoming like him in his death, if somehow I may attain the resurrection from the dead.
>
> Not that I have already obtained this or have already reached the goal; but I press on to make it my own, because Christ Jesus has made me his own. (Philippians 3:10-12)

About the Writing Team

Undoubtedly you've noticed by now that no one person wrote this book. We're a team of six writers. Two things we all have in common are that we love Jesus, and we work for InterVarsity Christian Fellowship. The similarities probably stop there! We are very different people, coming at the topic of this book from very different perspectives. That's a plus, not a minus.

Kevin and Jon are from Southern California. Robbie is from Tallahassee, by way of Reno. Amy lives in Normal (no wisecracks, please; we've already made them all), south of Chicago. Bobby resides in that quaint urban village New York City. I follow the Braves, America's baseball team, and their home is my home. Some of us have served as InterVarsity staff for a few years, others around twenty-five years. We're African American, Caucasian, Vietnamese American and Japanese American.

Before we started, some of us had never even met. As we twice holed ourselves up in the warm Atlanta home of David Scott, a long-time board member of InterVarsity, we shared our lives with each other. There is a healthy diversity of views on discipleship represented on our writing team. It clearly became a strength, not a weakness, as we dreamed up the content of this book and as we wrote, read and critiqued each other's chapters.

If you see some ideas in one chapter that seem to contradict ideas in another, you're probably right. We didn't want to write a book in which we agreed on every jot and tittle. (If we had, it never would have been written!) We do agree on the majors (like basic evangelical theology) but not necessarily on the minors. We hope you'll see that as a plus.

About the Book

We wrote with college-age to thirtyish young adults in mind. If this book proves to be a helpful discipleship resource for those younger or older than our target audience, that's great.

We designed the book to be used individually or in a discipling relationship or as a tool for small group discussion. Rather than dividing the content into larger chapters of fifteen to twenty pages, we chose instead to write twenty-four smaller chapters of seven to nine pages. We wanted a book that could be used as the basis for weekly discussions during a school year, having short chapters that would not overwhelm students with heavy academic loads or young professionals putting in sixty-hour workweeks.

The book is divided into three major sections. The first section (chapters 1-5) covers who we are "in Christ." The next section (chapters 6-13) deals with who we are "in relationship" with others. The final section (chapters 14-24) focuses on how we relate "in the world."

One cannot write everything there is to say on important areas of discipleship in seven to nine pages. So at the end of each chapter you'll find books we recommend for those who want to dig deeper.

Deciding what gets covered in a discipleship book and what gets left out was a tough task. As we chose content, we kept prefacing the discussions with: In what areas do *this generation and the next* most need to be developed as they seek to become mature followers of Jesus?

Our collective prayer is that we have hit the nail on the head for you. May you be encouraged to step out of your comfort zones and develop *Faith on the Edge.*

Living Your Faith

1. How did you come into a relationship with Jesus? Who and what helped you to come to a living faith?

2. Are you content with being a "decent little cottage" or would you rather become a "palace" where Jesus intends to come and live in it himself? Be as candid and honest as you can.

3. What stands in the way (relationships, priorities, dreams for your future, sins, for starters) of your becoming that palace?

4. Ask God to use this book to speak his truth powerfully into your life.

Recommended Reading

The Fight by John White, InterVarsity Press.

The Pursuit of God by A. W. Tozer, Christian Publications.

two

Gaining by Losing
Robbie Castleman

I HATE MY LIFE," MACK SAID, STARKLY SUMMARIZING HOW HE FELT to a group of friends. We chimed in immediately with comments like, "Well, hey, Mack, what's happened? What's wrong?" Mack continued, "Well, I don't know if anything is wrong, actually. I just hate my life, and that's pretty much how Jesus said things should be if I'm on the right track." I was relieved and annoyed. Mack was just being theological—probably just to get our attention. Well, he did get my attention for a long time after our conversation ended.

Why was Mack's comment so foreign to our ears? We knew Jesus said to his disciples, "Those who love their life lose it, and those who hate their life in this world will keep it for eternal life" (John 12:25). Even if this was true in my own life, until Mack spoke up I would never have used Jesus' language for my own.

It seems like there is something wrong with hating your life. But if this is a definition of what it means to be a follower of Jesus, just what does Jesus mean—especially if it leads to a life of joy and reward?

Mack's comment and Jesus' words paint a picture of biblical discipleship. "Hating your life in this world" has within it the radical dimension of discipleship that Jesus was always after. It's radical to suggest that the cost of discipleship is hating your own life in this world! It's not that a disciple's life lacks joy or pleasure, but Jesus meant what he said.

Losing Your Life

This statement of Jesus' occurs between two footwashings in the Gospel of John. The first is the washing of Jesus' feet by Mary of Bethany (John 12:1-8). She took a pound of costly perfume and anointed the feet of Jesus with it and then wiped his feet with her hair. Maybe it was partly the extravagance and comfort of that event that prompted Jesus to take off his outer garment, grab a towel and wash the dusty feet of his disciples just a short while later (John 13:1-20).

In between these two footwashings Jesus entered Jerusalem, greeted by the adoration of a multitude as he rode a young donkey. A little later Jesus described the cost of being a disciple—true disciples lose their lives. They hate their lives in this world so that the world might be saved.

Following Jesus means not getting to follow anyone else. It means serving him, making the choices he made, living out his life. It's not easy to lose your life and give it away in a world that tells us to save it and keep it. Risking such radical love and obedience is what it means to hate your life in this world. And it's a choice that makes you an obedient servant of Jesus, a true disciple. And it's a choice that leads to eternal honor.

> Those who love their life lose it, and those who hate their life in this world will keep it for eternal life. Whoever serves me must follow me, and where I am, there will my servant be also. Whoever serves me, the Father will honor. (John 12:25-26)

Choosing to be a disciple of Jesus means loving his life, taking it as our own and finding a surprising joy. It means loving God like Jesus did and knowing the perfect love of God that casts out fear. It means loving others like Jesus did. It means being loved joyfully, washed lovingly and promised clearly that it's worth it! It means living dangerously close to God, losing our life for others and hating our life enough to die for the sake of the gospel.

Losing Your Life to Live

Heart transplant patients understand the concept of losing life to find life. For eighteen years I was a critical-care nurse specialist. I cared for many patients with heart problems that needed radical treatment. Some of them believed their doctor's diagnosis, submitted to the recommended treatment and lived. In essence, *they hated their life enough to risk losing it by submitting to radical treatment.* Others denied the problem was as bad as it was. Ignoring symptoms, they didn't take proper medication and refused surgical treatment, and most of them, if not all of them, died. They loved their life too much to admit its limits.

It's a more desperate situation when dealing with our spiritual heart condition. Jesus is our best spiritual diagnostician. On our first visit to his "office" we hear him say, "You do not have what it takes to survive." In the New Testament terminology we are "poor in spirit." Indeed, we are "blessed" if we begin to believe this diagnosis of our spiritual condition (Matthew 5:3).

Some people believe it but choose to live with the malady. They know they're sick but deny they're too sick. They put off a return visit and party hardy. They push the limits and try alternative treatments when they feel bad, but they continue to love their life, such as it is. Others continue to listen to the Great Physician and hear him say, "You are so sick that you have no alternative but to submit to my treatment." This is heart-breaking news—in fact, the New Testament says these people are blessed if they "mourn" over the state of their spiritual health (Matthew 5:7). This goes beyond the recognition of spiritual ill-health—it causes deep sorrow.

One of the first steps in learning to hate your life is to let your heart break over the real condition of the human soul and spirit. People who mourn are those who take Jesus' diagnosis of the problem more seriously than how they happen to feel at the moment. To seek healing, wholeness and comfort, they ask Jesus about the cure.

The cure is not a quick fix or a symptom-covering pill. The cure is not the self-effort of a great diet and vigorous exercise. The cure is not even a bypass. The human heart is sick and dying; it must be *replaced*. The natural human heart is incapable of forever beating spiritually, so it must be replaced by a heart that will beat forever. And the donor heart is God's.

Now I've had heart patients fully convinced of the severity of their illness, heartbroken over the prognosis of death, who still refuse to submit to the cure. It's too radical—seems too risky—and it's too dangerous. But I've also had patients so desperate to "try anything" that they've submitted to a transplant operation even though they knew it was radical, risky and dangerous.

In terms of the spiritual life there are plenty of people fully convinced of their need and even grieving over their lives, but they still refuse the radical nature of the redeemed life. It can sound like, "If I become a Christian, I know I'd have to _____" (fill in the blank: quit sleeping around, stop bar-hopping with friends, end the affair, forgive my father, get off drugs, come clean with my boss, stop stealing from work, tell the truth). Many people love their lives too much to lose them—even if it means gaining the life of God. In the New Testament Jesus says people who are "meek" will be blessed (Matthew 5:5).

This exercise of meekness means a radical submission to the will of another. In this analogy, despite the danger, risk and radical nature of losing one's life to gain the life of God, it means believing the Great Physician and submitting to his treatment. And our own hearts won't survive the treatment. We must lose our hearts to gain the heart of God. In fact, the New Testament's promise for the "meek" is that they will inherit all that God has wanted for them from the beginning of time.

Being a disciple begins with this radical transplant—the conversion of our hearts, the submission of our wills and the surrender of our lives. Being a disciple is a process of learning to hate our lives. We acknowledge our own inability to make ourselves well. We allow that fact to drive us to a sorrow that leads us to surrender our whole selves to *God's only cure for the problem: the cross of Jesus Christ.*

Open Heart Surgery

On the cross the heart of Jesus stopped beating. At the cross our sick hearts are nailed to death. Paul explains it this way: "I have been crucified with Christ; and it is no longer I who live, but Christ lives in me; and the *life* which I now live in the flesh I live by faith in the Son of God, who loved me, and delivered Himself up for me" (Galatians 2:20 NASB).

The cross is God's operating table. The empty tomb is the "recovery room" where we rediscover our new life and wake up with new appetites. Because Jesus is alive, risen from the dead, his heart beats forever. This is the essential starting point of discipleship: his heart has supernaturally become our own.

The heart of Jesus beats forever because of *who* Jesus is—God among us. In Jesus, God became a human being in order to redeem our complete selves, body, soul, spirit. The incarnation, God-in-the-flesh, is the only explanation for the work and words of Jesus in the rest of the New Testament. If Jesus was not fully God and fully human, then the cross would have become a deathbed—for us as well as for Jesus. But God's sacrifice for us *in Jesus* works because God's life *in Jesus* left the tomb empty.

Every patient who has had a physical heart transplant will die. That "new" heart will stop beating some day. Not so in the kingdom of the Great Physician. Jesus' disciples wake up in the recovery room hungering and thirsting after the things God desires, namely, his righteousness (Matthew 5:6). Disciples leave the "hospital" so grateful for their health that they are especially merciful toward those who are still sick (Matthew 5:7). Disciples live out their days so grateful for God's heart replacing their own that they take on God's lifestyle, forsaking the habits of the heart that made them sick to begin with (Matthew 5:8). They engage other people who are in turmoil over their health and make every effort to introduce them to the Great Physician, who can do the same radical redemptive work for them (Matthew 5:9).

And disciples live out their days misunderstood because of the choice they made to undergo the "transplant." There are many others who refuse to take the risk of radical faith, and they revile and despise and persecute those who do. Disciples bear these charges with patience, persevere through prayer and return insult with blessing. It makes for a hard, misunderstood, lonely and, yes, hated life.

But *gladness* is its mark. Gladness because the former and now hated life is lost to gain the eternal life of reward and joy (Matthew 5:10-12). Gladness because *in Jesus* we are never alone, never abandoned, never left to our own resources, never the sole source to solve our own problems, never without hope, never without a future that is secure in the work and person and promise of God's Son, our Savior, Jesus Christ!

Extreme Discipleship

Jesus did not live the "balanced Christian life," and he didn't ask his disciples to "balance" their lives. Now, if what I mean by "balance" is mental healthiness, emotional stability and a deep trust that God is at work beyond what we can invest in a twenty-four-hour day, then Jesus is a model of balance. These are good traits, and if balance like this resulted from a disciple's deep dependence on God, I think it would look a lot like Jesus.

But too often *balance* is just another word for compromise, accommodation or selfishness. "Balance" can be a way of worshiping your life, an unwillingness deep down to really lose it for the kingdom. "Balance" often teaches us to juggle "God and worldly goods," "serve two masters" and accept anxiety as the price for being responsible. "Balance" is often nothing but a quest for social acceptance, economic security and a religious comfort zone. It is disobedience to the radical teachings of Jesus for his disciples.

Jesus lived a life completely sold out to God's will, radically given away to others and totally dependent on the Spirit. For the early followers of Jesus, being a disciple didn't look "balanced"—it looked fundamentally extreme, countercultural and radical to the core. Disciples hated their life because they loved Jesus. Disciples didn't strike a "balance"; they lost their lives to change the world, love the Lord and look like Jesus.

What does radical discipleship look like? In writing this chapter I thought about telling stories about well-known people who certainly lost their lives for the gospel. They are disciples fit for the "big screen" who have hated their lives enough to give them away for the sake of the gospel. We need people like this, and we need to hear their stories and learn from them how to answer the question, What would Jesus do?

But if we model our lives after "supersaints," we generally focus on the highlights of their lives that end up in print. We don't see the day-to-day obedience that is rather boring to hear about, that actually resulted in their testimonies.

I've read through nine years worth of diaries written by my husband's mother, who was a missionary in China during the 1930s. In nine years there are only recorded a few exciting episodes, only two or three pages that tell stories of bandits, baby rescues, threats to her life and faithful stands for the gospel that would end up as public stories to tell. The rest of her diary reads like mine. She tries to trust the Lord for the price of food; she prays for friends; she mentions people she meets and her attempts to share with them; she bemoans her menstrual cramps; she confesses her lack of gratitude; she struggles with serving her coworkers; she hopes and prays for progress in her work. For every moment of invigorating victory, she has days, weeks, months and even years of plain faithfulness in giving her life away.

Discipleship, for the most part, isn't real exciting. It's worthwhile. It's valued by God but seldom noticed by people. It's quiet, increasingly steady and invariably costly. Discipleship has just as much to do with how we take an interest in our parents as it does praying for the salvation of Muslims. Discipleship has just as much to do with means as with ends—just as much to do with the journey as it does with the destination. Discipleship that results in a lifetime marked by obedience happens because of minute-by-minute decisions of faithfulness.

Discipleship is just as radical when we choose not to slam a door as when we open our door to a needy person. It doesn't happen "over there"; it can only happen where you choose to be obedient to Jesus. Discipleship doesn't happen "when the time is right"; it can only happen in the very moment you are living. It doesn't wait until "everything is ready"; it happens when we are ready to lose our lives, hate our lives, for the sake of following Jesus step by step, left foot, right foot, left foot, right foot.

Disciples share in the glory of Jesus because they take up the cross of Jesus and follow him to Calvary in order to get to the empty tomb. Being a Christian means willingly embracing a life that includes suffering, *the loss of yourself as the focus of satisfaction*. Discipleship means following Jesus, who "endured the cross and despised the shame" because the journey ends joyfully in the presence of God (Hebrews 12:2).

Discipleship is living out the life of the heart Donor—day by day, minute by minute, following Jesus in the way of suffering to share his glory (Romans 8:17). Dietrich Bonhoeffer, a German theologian who resisted the Nazis, wrote:

> If our Christianity has ceased to be serious about discipleship, if we have watered down the gospel into emotional uplift which makes no costly demands and which fails to distinguish between natural and Christian existence, then . . . [being despised and rejected like Jesus] has ceased to be intelligible to a Christianity which can no longer see any difference between an ordinary human life and the life committed to Christ. *(The Cost of Discipleship)*

In a day when the church, not to mention our culture, is more concerned about happiness than holiness, the words of Jesus that we should hate our lives and lose our lives sound ill-advised. But following Jesus has always been ill-advised for people who love their lives and want a comfortable and predictable lifetime. Discipleship is not for the faint of heart—it's dangerous! It's on the edge! Dangerous discipleship is only for people with a heart that is guaranteed to beat forever. Disciples have nothing to lose in this world, so they risk it all. Disciples are people who joyfully hate their lives for the sake of loving Jesus.

Living Your Faith

1. Look up the Beatitudes in Matthew 5:3-12. If you are a disciple, how did your initial encounter with the gospel compare to Jesus' summary? If you have not yet trusted God radically, where would you place yourself in Jesus' description of becoming a disciple? You may want to reread pages 22 to 25 in this chapter for an explanation of the Beatitudes.

2. "For the early followers of Jesus being a disciple didn't look 'balanced'—it looked fundamentally extreme, countercultural and radical to the core." In what way does that describe your life? In what areas does your life conform to other expectations, dreams or standards?

3. What are one or two things you can do for others that will significantly cost you (time, money, effort, status) as a disciple?

4. For further reflection on the meaning of the incarnation read J. I. Packer's *Knowing God*, C. S. Lewis' *Mere Christianity* or John Stott's *Basic Christianity* with a friend.

5. Read Dietrich Bonhoeffer's *The Cost of Discipleship* as part of a small group.

Recommended Reading

The Cost of Discipleship by Dietrich Bonhoeffer, Collier.

A Long Obedience in the Same Direction by Eugene Peterson, InterVarsity Press.

three

The Healing Journey

Jonathan Tran

MAY 5, 1977, WAS MY OLDEST BROTHER'S TENTH BIRTHDAY. THE whole family eagerly prepared a Vietnamese feast for his party. Before the festivities my other brother, six-year-old David, and I (five years old) decided to play out in the front yard. David spotted a beautiful rose garden across the street. "Wouldn't it be great to get some for Mommy?" Good idea! Mom could proudly display a sign of her sons' affection for all to see tonight, we thought.

Our plan was simple yet brilliant—we would carefully assemble a bouquet of roses by making several trips, taking only a couple roses at a time as to not raise any suspicion. Like two ninjas, David and I darted across the street, tore a few roses off the bush and darted back. We made several successful forays into enemy territory, bringing back the spoils. We were soon on our way to a beautiful bouquet and Mom's glowing pride. Then it happened, right in front of me.

I never saw the car. I am sure David never saw the car. A series of images: an ambulance, a police officer placing a chair over David's body to slow down approaching traffic, everyone weeping. I played fireman, running throughout the house, frolicking between suffering people. I had no idea. I saw it from inches away, yet I did not know what death was. I would not talk about that day for fifteen years.

I follow Jesus because I need healing. My obedience isn't about being religious, noble or good. Jesus said that he came not for the righteous but for the sick. I am not righteous. I am sick. I need him to do things in my life that I cannot. I need him because I am a broken, wounded, wounding person. Every day I need him to give me a clue about how to live life. I need him to show me how to treat others with decency and goodness. I need him to guide my life, to give me hope. I need him to encourage me along the journey, to pick me up when I fall down. I am glad Jesus came for the sick because he came for me.

The Healing Process

Healing is a journey. Just as folks in the Gospels pursued God for healing, so must we. The leper, the blind man, Jairus whose daughter was dying, the bleeding woman—they all pursued Jesus. For each of them there was a time of suffering, an element of hoping and a place where God restored wholeness. Mostly there was a pursuit of the Good Doctor Jesus, a stubborn belief that he alone could cure them.

We need the Good Doctor to do some healing in our lives. For some that means physical healing of colds, broken limbs and cancers. For all of us that means emotional redemption from past sins done to us or by us. There are many places in our family histories, our relationships and our world where things have been done poorly, leaving scars. In the Gospels, the journey of healing is a dynamic relationship between Jesus and the sick.

Identity, obedience, vulnerability, community, faith and witness are parts of this healing journey.

Identity: Do You Want to Be Healed?

In John 5 Jesus approaches a man sitting near the healing pool of Bethesda. The man had been an invalid for thirty-eight years. Jesus approaches him and asks, "Do you want to healed?" The question might seem absurd—of course the man wants to be healed! But Jesus is on to something profound. For thirty-eight years the only world the man has known is his own sickness. He identifies with it. It is who he is: a sick man. He struggles with changing his identity from a sick man to a healed man. Leaving the old identity would be difficult. He points to the difficulty he has had getting to the pool. He is not able to recognize the Good Doctor in front of him. He focuses, instead, on his own suffering.

Many of us, crippled by those we trusted, have the identity of wounded people. Certainly, embracing our woundedness and brokenness exhibits a healthy, practical theology of our fallenness. However, our identity is more than just wounded, broken or fallen people. We are also healed, transformed and redeemed.

Yet rather than embracing our brokenness for the sake of redemption, we embrace it as our identity. We understand ourselves in terms of our sickness and wounds. Some might say, "I am a child of divorce." "I am a sexual-abuse victim." "I am a product of racism." Those statements may be true, but they are not the whole story. For every victim of divorce, abuse and racism, there is an opportunity for healing and for bringing glory to God.

After my brother David died, I was alone. My loneliness was exacerbated by moving fifteen times. As soon as I made new friends and began to develop intimacy and trust, we moved again. I learned to rely on myself. I had friendships but trusted no one. I resigned myself to being alone. I got involved in a campus fellowship where I had friendships and even ministered to others. Yet in my four years there, I trusted very few. My constant internal lament was, *No one knows me.* But I was not exactly open to intimacy. I presented myself in such a way that others couldn't get to know me or wouldn't want to get to know me. I also created an impossibly high bar for "knowing me." No one could know me as I defined it. So no one did.

I was stubbornly holding on to my identity as a lonely person. I blamed everyone for my loneliness. Even as Jesus brought others to me, I remained guarded. He was asking, "Do you want to be healed?" I was saying no, complaining that the pool of intimacy was so far away. I rejected the healing Jesus offered. I ignored those he brought and held tightly to my identity as a sick person.

Obedience: Take Up Your Mat and Walk

Healing does not happen by sitting around on a comfortable hospital bed while the Good Doctor administers medication intravenously. It requires God's goodness *and* our obedience.

In Mark 2 Jesus is teaching in a crowded room. Lowered through the roof by ambitious friends, a paralyzed man is placed at Jesus' feet. Jesus commands the man, "Take up your mat and walk." Considering his authority and the man's desire to be whole, the anticipated response may seem obvious. Any paralyzed person who wants to walk is going to obey, right? But imagine yourself as a paralyzed person. Jesus is asking you to do something you have never done before, or at least not in a very long time. What if you try and your body doesn't respond, or you get up only to fall down in front of a crowd? What if you have forgotten how to walk? Yet without obeying Jesus' simple command, this man can never walk again. No matter how much Jesus does for him or how loyal his friends are, the definitive step is his. He must obey the Good Doctor to be healed.

This is also true for us. Jesus heals through his cross, the Bible, the Spirit and his church, yet we need to do what he commands. The diagnosis for health is always accompanied by a prescription. Before Jesus heals you from the pain of racism, you may need to obey him by pursuing relationships with the very ethnic group that wounded you. In being healed from sexual abuse, God may very well prescribe that you forgive the very person who abused you. In healing from your parents' nasty divorce, you may have to love them. The healing journey requires obedience.

Jesus' commandment for me was simple, "Get up and trust some people. Let yourself be known. Quit hiding behind ministry and build some deep relationships." As I allowed others in, as I lowered my expectations (demands) of friendship and intimacy, I began to heal.

What is Jesus calling you to do in order to be healed? What risks are there? Confess your fears and complaints to God, and ask him to help you do what you need to do. Watch and see what happens.

Vulnerability: Telling Your Whole Story

For most of us, few others know our deepest wounds. Often the stories are so painful or sordid that we may not be able to or want to recall them. Silence is a potent barrier to healing. Jesus wants to hear your story.

In Mark 5 Jesus is touched by a woman who has been suffering from an ongoing menstrual period for twelve years. Twelve years! Imagine all the cramping, discomfort, physical weariness and emotional upheaval of a one-week period. Now imagine the suffering from a twelve-year menstruation. Further, the woman's suffering was aggravated by many doctors who had tricked her for years. Fearing rejection, the woman sneaks up to Jesus in the middle of a huge, pushing crowd, gently touching the bottom of his cloak. Immediately the bleeding stops. She is healed without inconveniencing or contaminating the Good Doctor. Yet Jesus stops and seeks the person who touched him.

The woman comes trembling before him. Fearing harsh rebuke, she cowers at his feet. Instead of admonishment, Jesus offers a kind ear as she gives him "the whole story" (Mark 5:33 The Message).

I began my healing process with a journal. I knew there were things in my life that plagued me. I filled my journal with writing, art, newspaper clippings, manuscript Bible-study sheets, song lyrics, quotes from books, letters to God and everything else that God showed me. My story is in that journal—everything about my life away from God and my healing by God. That journal is a testament to my sin and Jesus' grace.

I began counseling and speaking openly about my issues. What had been hidden by fear and shame was now in the open. I was no longer held by the fear of what others thought of me.

You too need to tell your story. As much as you do not even want to think about the sexual abuse, you need to recount it to Jesus—tell him about it—ask him to take it to the cross so that the evil of it dies there.

You need to tell others about the racist things people did to you. You need to speak openly without shame. This may mean standing up at a Bible study and sharing your pain with others. It may mean seeing a counselor, recounting the experience many times. It may mean sharing with your prayer partner.

Community: The Paralytic Was Carried by Four Friends

Healing happens in community—involving other people. Remember the paralytic carried on a stretcher to Jesus (Mark 2)? Undeterred by the huge crowd in the packed house, the friends take the paralytic to the roof. They create a hole in the roof through which they gingerly lower their friend to Jesus' feet. When he "saw their faith," Jesus was impressed.

As we pursue healing, we need to be surrounded by a group of people who pray, ask hard questions and serve in practical ways. The healing process can be exhausting. We need our spiritual community to carry us and put us at Jesus' feet.

During my healing process, my community was my housemates. Tom and Denise, Mario, and I met each Monday. Together we read books on healing and spiritual bondage. When I wanted to abandon the process or stray from the Good Doctor, they encouraged me to be faithful. They carried me through the most difficult times. It was this community that carried me to Jesus. They were not deterred by my condition. I believe that Jesus saw the faith of my community as much as he saw mine.

Faith: Do Not Fear, Only Believe

As we consider our woundedness, many of us are scared. We are scared of facing the pain of our past. We are scared of having others know that we don't have it all together. We are scared that our sickness will be with us for our whole lives.

In Mark 5 Jairus, a synagogue ruler who had begged Jesus to save his twelve-year-old daughter's life, finds out that his daughter is dead. Yet Jesus says, "Do not fear, only believe." And the daughter is healed.

In the darkest parts of the healing journey, we can be sure that Jesus still is with us. No matter how protracted the abuse or how messy the divorce, Jesus can handle it. He is able to come into our lives and tell us that what seems like death is not as bad as we thought (not because the suffering is not bad but because Jesus is able to redeem it). He is able to heal us of any condition—sickness, anger, fear, loneliness, jealousy, abuse. Our part is to aggressively seek healing. Jesus will do what he's going to do in his own way and at the best time. Too often we find ourselves throwing our hands in the air and saying, "Forget it! Jesus can't help me."

The biggest barrier to my own healing was believing that Jesus could not change me. I saw that Jesus healed others, but it was hard to believe that Jesus would heal me. My healing required faith. My willingness to work hard, to drive an hour to see my counselor, to submit to the advice of my community, to abstain from certain behaviors, depended on whether I believed Jesus was going to do something. Jesus' words were simply, "Do not fear; only believe." In time Jesus changed me. Some of my greatest temptations began to subside. My identity slowly changed. Loneliness was replaced with intimacy. I was no longer afraid to deal with myself. *Jesus was healing me.*

Do you believe Jesus can change you?

Witness: I Was Blind, Now I See

As Jesus heals, we can go forth and tell others about it. We offer the world our stories about what God has done for us. This brings God glory, evidence of his awesome power on earth.

In John 9 Jesus encounters a man born blind. Jesus puts mud and spit on his eyes (healing is messy!) and the man is able to see. Afterward, he goes about telling people, "I was blind, now I see."

God heals us because he has a profound interest in his glory and our joy. When Jesus heals us of sexual abuse, we are released into joy and freedom. When Jesus heals us from abandonment, we are released to give ourselves more fully to others. When we stand before others to tell how God has healed us from the wounds of racism and proclaim God's power at work, people are confronted with the validity of Jesus.

Jesus has done a remarkable thing in my life; it is my greatest apologetic for faith. I believe what Jesus did in my life, he can do in yours. I was sick, but now I am well.

Living Your Faith

1. In what ways are you holding on to your identity as a sick and wounded person?

2. In what forum (your Bible study, small group, prayer partnership,

family) can you break the power of shame by telling your whole story?

3. In your healing process, who is your community? How are they helping you through this time?

4. How are you demonstrating and proclaiming Jesus' goodness to you?

5. How can you tell your story to help others consider Jesus?

Recommended Reading

Healing for Broken People (Global Issues Bible Studies) by Dan Harrison, InterVarsity Press.

Inner Healing by Mike Flynn and Doug Gregg, InterVarsity Press.

Life Recovery Guides (three study guides on recovery from abuse, depression and family dysfunctions) by Dale and Juanita Ryan, InterVarsity Press.

four

Dangerous Truth
for the Daring Life
Robbie Castleman

O UR CHILD DIED—THAT'S HOW IT ALL BEGAN."
A chemistry professor speaking on a state university campus
had just concluded a brilliant multipoint presentation of why he
found Christianity credible. After the presentation I asked him what first
motivated his investigation of the Christian faith. He responded by saying it
began with the death of his child. Many months after this tragic loss, he
noticed his wife's grief began to give way to some hope and healing, which
eluded him. When he asked her about it, she confessed that she had been
attending a Bible study with friends and had become a Christian. He was
surprised, intrigued and open to anything that would comfort his pain and
emptiness.

This new group of friends opened their hearts and the Scriptures to this
professor and his wife. He felt free to ask questions, seek the truth of the
Christian faith, express doubts and finally trust the Lord because his feelings of grief were accepted and shared. Empathy preceded answers. Grace
opened the door of truth for him and his wife. This is true in the hearts and

lives of most people who need to hear the gospel.

Jesus is the perfect friend. He is full of grace and truth (John 1:14). His grace opened the door of truth to many. He refused to cast a stone and then told a woman to "sin no more" (John 8:1-11). He drew crowds by healing and then preached the kingdom message. Jesus began his most famous sermon with the grace of the Beatitudes before the truth commands of righteousness (Matthew 5—7). *Grace moved the Savior close to people. Truth then moved them close to him.*

The Gospel Is Both Grace and Truth

Being "full of grace and truth" is not easy for any of us. Our problem is that we usually have more of one than the other. We are full of truth and answer questions that haven't been asked; we preach to people who just want to talk; and we reduce the gospel to an outline of the facts. Or we are so full of grace that we never risk sharing the gospel's exclusive claims in a way that people can hear the radical distinction the truth of the gospel demands in our lives.

It's important that we share the truth in a way that gives grace enough time to work. This happens when we believe the Lord has already been at work in a friend's life. This trust is more important than our own presentation, knowledge or training. Grace helps us wait and listen to a person until we hear the question behind the comment, feel the hurt under the protest or see the place where faith can grow.

Friends who speak the truth at the right time are confident that the power of the gospel alone can reach the heart to save (Romans 1:16). The saving, central issues of the gospel are the person, death and resurrection of Jesus Christ. Our confidence in his work must overwhelm any tendency we have to make the "foolishness" of the gospel sound "wise" (1 Corinthians 1:18-25).

What is the good news that is powerful to save, heal and transform a person's life? It is bound up in the person and work of Jesus. It is not the story of how I came to believe that saves another person; it is the gospel within my story that contains the power of God. So when I share with others *how* I came to believe, the important part of what I share is *what* I came to believe, the gospel. The particulars of my story are only the setting for the gospel's priceless jewel.

The Truth of the Gospel

The gospel is good news because it is honest about the bad news, and the bad news is really bad—especially for Jesus. On the night Jesus was betrayed, he prayed in the garden, "Father, if it is possible let this cup pass from me." Jesus wanted to be the means of redemption, to bear away the sin of the world (John 1:29), but he didn't want to die if he didn't have to. God the Father had bad news for God the Son that night. A different cup, a different way of redemption, was not possible.

The sacrificial death of the sinless Son of God was the only way to conquer sin and death once and for all. Only Jesus, through his suffering and death on the cross, could bear all wrong and rebellion, all suffering and sadness, all brokenness and evil, and overcome it by his perfect goodness and absolute sacrifice. If there had been any other way, surely the Father would have said "yes" to his Son's prayer. But this would have meant a "no" to us. Sin-filled and rebellious people would have been left without hope for redemption. God said "no" to Jesus to say "yes" to us. There is no salvation apart from the cross of the incarnate God, Jesus Christ.

Sometimes I wish—just like Jesus in the garden—that there had been another way: light so many candles, say so many prayers, do so many good deeds, believe something completely and sincerely, and don't hurt anybody else. I wish eternal salvation could be found in all belief systems, world religions or sincere efforts. But it isn't. Christians know it isn't so because of the cross. If God didn't say "okay, I'll think of something else" to his perfect, sinless and beloved Son, then God certainly won't say it to anyone else. If there is salvation outside the person and work of Jesus Christ, then the cross is a cruel joke, the misguided effort of a wannabe messiah. Throughout the New Testament Jesus is identified as the singular means to a relationship with God (John 1:12; 14:6; Acts 4:12; 1 John 5:11-12).

The truth is either defined by the cross in all its exclusivity and power, or there is no truth and there is no salvation. We are lost forever, left to ourselves and subject to unmediated sin and unmitigated evil. People who protest that the cross of Jesus as "the only way" is intolerant, narrow-minded and exclusive are often the same people who protest the evil, injustice and pain in the world.

But only the suffering and death of the sinless God-man, Jesus Christ, takes what's wrong with the world seriously. The cross-laden gospel of Christianity takes evil so seriously that God-in-Christ must provide the only, final and adequately redemptive answer in his own death. Then God proves the effectiveness of Christ's work on the cross by overcoming death. The cross without the resurrection is nothing but a "nice try." The cross with the resurrection is the only hope of the world.

Disciples embrace this truth gratefully and humbly. The truth is not a weapon but a *way*. The truth doesn't keep people out; it invites people in. The truth isn't easy to hear and is even harder to believe, but it doesn't bend to personal preference or accommodate to the culture. The truth is the truth because everything else is defined by it. There was no other "cup" for Jesus because there is no other means of salvation. Disciples tell people the truth of the gospel because it is full of grace.

And the gospel makes sense of everything else. On a plane I once sat next to a East European who was finishing a postdoc in physics. When he asked what I did ("I teach the Bible") his eyes lit up and he said, "Oh this is so interesting to me. I would like to ask you a question." I said, "Sure!" expecting that he was going to ask me something about the age of the earth, Noah's flood or why there are so many denominations. But he asked me a real question—a question of the heart that his mind and his research couldn't answer. He asked, "Do you think the universe has meaning?"

What a wonderful question! And it was great to have a wonderful answer. Our conversation naturally led to the person and work of the God-man, Jesus Christ, and his interest grew. He thanked me for listening to him and for answering his question. He lamented, "I can't talk to anyone in my department or at the lab about questions of 'meaning.' That isn't allowed, but I just know it all has to mean something or what's the point?" The exclusive claims of God's truth said clearly in grace make the gospel's power compelling.

The Grace of the Gospel

A friendship fostered by grace can risk telling the truth. With Jesus as our model, how does grace and truth look as we encounter people in the secular world today? It looks more like a personal relationship than a religious program. Distorted caricatures of Christianity promoted by both religious and secular media are harder to dislodge from people hardened by fraudulent displays of the truth in culture, country and church.

Traditional evangelistic methods like booklet gospel presentations, mass-appeal events or even door-to-door campaigns are only appropriate for a very small percentage of seekers. The astonishing lack of biblical knowledge and concepts creates a greater challenge for making the Christian faith clear. People are wary of being "sold" someone else's goods. And the exclusivity of Jesus as God incarnate, as well as the cross and resurrection, sound intolerant and rigid in a world addicted to relativism and feel-good religious franchises.

Using Jesus' teaching in Luke 8:4-15, we need "good soil" for the "seed" of God's Word to take root and grow in people's lives today. "Good soil" that can receive the Word-seed is hard to find in today's workplace, college campus or a neighbor's living room. Disciples need to sow the truth-seed widely and hopefully, with joy and grace.

In our witness to the reality of the grace and truth of Jesus, we have to accept the process of "weed killing," "rock moving" and "ground plowing" to prepare a place for the seed of the Word to grow in "good soil." We also must pray in order to keep the stealing "birds" away. If we are confident that God is at work beyond our efforts, we can afford to work, watch and pray.

The Gospel Is God's Truth About His Grace

I live in a part of the Bible belt where sharing the good news often begins with people who are aware of basic Bible facts but have little understanding of the gospel's implications. Jesus can be on a car's bumper sticker yet have nothing to do with the driver's family life or business affairs. Addressing the lordship of Christ and issues of lifestyle with these people requires much prayer and the development of trusting friendships. It takes time to reintroduce people to the Jesus they haven't truly known.

Sharing the gospel brings the privilege of being close enough to others to see the reality of God's faith-creating work (Ephesians 2:8-9). Prayerfully watching a person's response to the gospel as it is shared over time is an important part of being a disciple. Listening to a person's heart behind the words, doubts behind the questions, fears behind the objections, search behind the evasion, is critically important. How else can we be prepared to speak a good word at the right time (Proverbs 15:23)? Part of being a disciple is knowing how to pray for a particular person, how to socialize with them as well as how to relate the gospel's truth clearly.

On the other hand, there are people who have been so isolated from the person and work of Jesus that on hearing the good news, Christ captures their attention and they quickly surrender to the gospel. We don't know what God has been doing behind the scenes to stir up a person's life! I know of people who have genuinely come to Christ in a single conversation and others who have taken years to make the same decision. In both cases God was the ultimate evangelist, and this is where our confidence lies.

This must be our source of confidence if we are to be patient enough that people don't become mere projects. Sharing the good news is not a program with a "success or failure" end. God is faithful. Scripture reassures us that no one who belongs to the Father will be lost (John 17:12) and that those who belong to him have been known by him since before the foundations of the world (Ephesians 1:4). He seeks the lost (Luke 15) and desires that none perish (John 3:16; 10:28). Having God's loving, seeking, compassionate *grace* can help people hear the *truth* of the gospel, the exclusive claims of the cross and resurrection of Jesus with more openness. If we are really convinced of God's love for the lost, telling the truth becomes a work of grace.

Disciples are not burdened with "saving" people. God goes before us to help prepare the good soil for his own Word. And God's Word will not "return . . . empty, but it shall accomplish that which [God] purpose[s]." In this passage from Isaiah 55, the Word uses the imagery of the harvest to reflect the faithfulness of God when "results" are unseen for a time.

For as the rain and the snow come down from heaven,
and do not return there until they have watered

the earth,
making it bring forth and sprout,
    giving seed to the sower and bread
        to the eater,
so shall my word be that goes out from my mouth;
    it shall not return to me empty. (Isaiah 55:10-11)

No one can predict the time frame of another's journey "out of darkness and into his marvelous light" (1 Peter 2:9). But it is a special joy to see some come to full harvest in a single season. I've seen students leave college after four years of being surrounded by faithful Christian friends and still not come to faith in Christ. I've seen others who started off without any knowledge of the Bible or without having heard of Jesus surrender their hearts to the gospel in a single semester. I've known people who sat in church their whole lives and through a sermon, a hymn, a special program or a poignant need suddenly realized they have never really surrendered their lives to the gift and demand of God in the gospel.

Our job is to tell it well. Tell it well after listening well. Tell it clearly after understanding it ourselves. Tell it truthfully because it is not our's to corrupt. Tell it with conviction because it doesn't accommodate tolerance that includes untruth. Tell it with grace because it has saved our own lives. Tell it honestly and humbly because the gospel is good—it is not a weapon of self-defense or self-justification. Tell it often because there is salvation nowhere else, in no one else but the Lord Jesus.

Cultish legalism wounds people with guilt because it lacks grace. Even truth can be used as a weapon when dysfunctional family dynamics make the gospel anything but good news. Wounded seekers need time to discern the difference between what they have experienced and the gospel which is full of grace and truth. Seeing the difference between religion and a relationship with a loving God can begin with friends who are willing to simply have fun together. Learning to trust people, let alone God, can take some time. Learning to be trustworthy in a friendship can be the very best way to love the spiritually wounded and the lost.

The Gospel Is Good News

Listening and asking questions can be the gospel's germination of grace in the good soil of a person's heart. Speaking the truth in love and in the language of everyday life lets the power of the gospel bring the seed to full bloom. The thoughtful courtesies of life can help us be good evangelists. Our confidence in God's unseen work can help make us patient and prayerful. Gratitude for our own salvation can make us faithful. And grace-filled faithfulness to the difficult and exclusive truth claims of the gospel makes us disciples of *Jesus*—and no one else.

Living Your Faith

1. How did you come to believe the truth and grace of the gospel? (Think of a specific time and place and who it was who shared with you.)

How has your life changed because of your redemption in Christ?

What is God still transforming in your life?

2. Think about the garden of Gethsemane and the cross of Jesus. Reflect on how they give evidence to the necessity of Christ's work alone for salvation. Who do you find it most difficult to make this clear to, and why?

3. Write out the good news of the gospel, including the cross and resurrection, in four or five sentences. Try to use "nonchurchy" words for what is meant by "sin," "repentance," "redemption" and so on.

4. Pray for people who need to hear your story (#1 above) and the good news (#2 above). Ask someone to join you in prayer for these people and your opportunity to share the good news with them.

Recommended Reading

Know the Truth by Bruce Milne, InterVarsity Press.

Know What You Believe by Paul Little, Chariot Victor.

five

Connecting with Jesus
Bobby Gross

WHEN I WAS A SMALL BOY, I READ OVER AND OVER THE LITTLE PIC-
ture book *If Jesus Came to My House*. It pictures a young Jesus
coming to visit a modern little boy, and they talk and play and have
tea together. As a child I was fascinated by the idea of meeting Jesus face to
face. In a sense, I still am. I envy the first-century women and men who knew
Jesus in the flesh. What would it be like to listen firsthand to his teaching, to ask
him my questions, to experience his miracles, to hang out with him as a friend,
to be, in the words of Peter, "an eyewitness of his majesty"?

Obviously Jesus is no longer physically present on earth, yet we have his
powerful promises: "Remember, I am with you always, to the end of the age,"
and "Where two or three are gathered in my name, I am there among them"
(Matthew 28:20; 18:20). How then do we experience the presence of Jesus?
How do we actually connect with him and grow in a relationship with him?

The Unrecognized Companion
In the final chapter of his Gospel, Luke tells an intriguing story that serves

as a paradigm for how we can encounter the Lord. At dawn a group of women come to the tomb of Jesus with spices for his tortured, lifeless body. But he is not there. Two angels declare that he has risen, and the women race to tell the other disciples, who foolishly discount the women's report as "an idle tale." Later that day, two of the disciples are walking the seven miles to a village called Emmaus. Disappointment and confusion are written all over their faces. Jesus is gone. The man they had believed and followed and grown to love was dead. How could this happen? Where was God?

"While they were talking and discussing, Jesus himself came near and went with them, but their eyes were kept from recognizing him" (Luke 24:15-16). From this passage we gain two important insights right away, one a comfort, the other a puzzle. First, *Jesus takes the initiative to come to us.* Of course, he came to us grandly in his incarnation in history, but he also comes to us in our daily experience. Primarily, *he* seeks *us* out and not the other way around. Even our seeking of God, we realize in retrospect, is prompted in some way by his initiative toward us. He does not play hard-to-get but comes to walk alongside us, especially in our times of need. This is grace.

The second insight is puzzling: *we do not always recognize his presence.* Sometimes, for his own wise purposes, Jesus keeps us from a full awareness of his nearness. Perhaps you have felt desperately alone at times, as though God were a million miles away. I don't understand why this is so, but I do know that God does not abandon us. In such times, we simply cling to this conviction. More often, though, the lack of recognition stems from us, for example, from our preoccupation with ourselves or our distraction by many concerns or our hardness of heart. Nonetheless, God is patiently present with us and willing to reveal himself, in time.

Jesus asks the two travelers what they are discussing. They are amazed that he seems unaware of the recent things that had taken place. "What things?" asks Jesus. He then listens as the two pour out their hearts. They tell what happened, they voice their hopes and disappointments, they acknowledge their uncertainties, and they say how they feel. Jesus listens. In effect, they are *praying* to Jesus. Basically, in prayer God invites us to freely speak our minds and hearts to him. Although he already knows them, he wants to hear these things from us in our own words. He listens.

Jesus responds to the travelers. He gently rebukes them, he provides a word of spiritual insight, and then, significantly, he speaks to them from the Scriptures: "Then beginning with Moses and the prophets, he interpreted to them the things about himself in all the scriptures" (Luke 24:27). *We encounter God through the Bible.* God can speak or reveal himself to us in many ways—through creation, through the Spirit, through people, through dreams, through angels—but foundationally, he has spoken through "the apostles and prophets," that is, the written Scriptures we call the Bible. Supremely, of course, he has spoken through his Son, incarnate in human history. That is why, as we learn from Jesus' on-the-road Bible study, all the Scriptures point to him. Later, the two exclaim, "Were not our hearts burning within us while he was talking to us on the road, while he was opening the scriptures to us?" (Luke 24:32). Like them, we experience the presence of God as we are immersed in his written Word.

When the travelers reach Emmaus, Jesus acts as if he is going on, but they urge him to stay with them overnight. Jesus agrees. At the dinner table he takes bread, blesses it, breaks it and gives it to them. "Then their eyes were opened and they recognized him; and he vanished from their sight" (Luke 24:30-31). Curiously, it seems that Jesus would have gone on had the disciples not invited him to stay. This suggests that our response to Jesus— our eagerness to be with him longer, to learn more from him—makes a difference. Seemingly, there are varying degrees of awareness of his presence. More importantly, we see here the significance of *fellowship* as a setting for "seeing" Jesus. When we gather with fellow believers, especially for the sharing in the eucharistic meal—the bread and wine representing the body and blood of Jesus—we experience his presence in a special way.

As Luke 24 concludes, we detect a further element in the paradigm. Again Jesus comes, this time to a larger group. The disciples are filled with joy and amazement. He further opens their minds to understand the Scriptures and reinforces their mission to be his witnesses in the world. Finally, at the point of his ascension he blesses those assembled and they worship him. In a distinctive way we too encounter Jesus when we gather for joyful *worship.*

Luke 24, then, gives us four important means by which Jesus meets us and reveals himself to us: prayer, Scripture, fellowship and worship. Indeed, we find these very elements emphasized in Luke's summary description of the life of the early church (Acts 2:42). Prominent in the book of Acts is the role of the Holy Spirit through whom the presence of Jesus continues, just as he promised (John 14:16-17, 23). In fact, the Spirit is active in each of the four dimensions above: he helps us in our praying (Romans 8:26-27), he enlightens us to understand Scripture (2 Peter 1:20-21), he unites us into one fellowship (Ephesians 4:3-6), and he inspires us to worship the Lord (John 4:23-24). So whenever we speak of knowing God or following Jesus, we are also speaking of the Holy Spirit by whom the Father and the Son have come to us and live within us. Let's examine in more detail how we can connect to Jesus through prayer and Scripture. (The other two "means," fellowship and worship, are covered in chapters seven through eleven.)

Prayer

Jesus prayed. He prayed in order to maintain a vital connection with the Father. Jesus' friends observed the regularity of his prayer and sometimes the intensity, as when he prayed all night. They saw him pray alone, pray with others in small clusters and pray publicly in the synagogue. They heard him expressing praise, reciting the psalms, interceding for others and agonizing over God's will. Once, after Jesus finished a time of prayer, one of his friends asked him to teach the group to pray. Jesus gave them the following pattern for prayer. It is known today as the Lord's Prayer but might better be called "the disciples' prayer" (Luke 11:1-4).

We approach God as Father. Jesus teaches us to address God as "Abba," a familial name something like "Papa." Jesus wants us to identify with him as the Son and along with him to enter into an intimacy with his Father. God is True Father to us, not like our own earthly fathers, even at their best. He loves us unconditionally. We are free to approach him with confidence, but not with flippancy or disrespect. After all, he is our Father *enthroned in heaven*, the very Creator of the cosmos.

We show respect for who God is. We "hallow" or treat as holy his name.

We acknowledge that he is "other" than us, set apart, wholly pure and just, full of glory. We honor him by expressing praise, by giving thanks, by offering worship.

We express our allegiance to God's purposes. We long to see more and more people submit to his rightful leadership. We want to see his goodness and justice increasingly prevail in our society and the nations of the world. We want to see the church growing in size and effectiveness. We want to see more of our own lives changed and conformed to his ways. We want his kingdom to come and his will to be done on earth as it is in heaven.

We depend on God for all of our needs. Only now do we turn to ourselves in the pattern. We look to God for "daily bread," which in its largest sense means all that is necessary to live our lives with contentment, starting with our food. We should remember each day that our very breath is a gift from God.

We look to God for forgiveness and grace. Here, we acknowledge before God all the ways we have defied him and fallen short of his expectations. We admit the things we've done and the things we've left undone. We confess our failure to love him wholeheartedly or our neighbors as ourselves. We ask his forgiveness. At the same time we take inventory of who *we* need to forgive and ask his grace to do so. Our experience of forgiveness is linked to our willingness to forgive.

We trust him to lead and protect us. We ask that we not be brought to a time of trial where our faith will be subjected to hardship or temptation. Yet we know that we aren't always exempt from such times, so we add another request that we would be delivered from the evil one. We look to God to guide us and guard us as we live our daily lives.

This is the pattern Jesus has given us. There are many other patterns available to us, for example, the psalms of the Old Testament or the prayers in the letters of the New Testament. But this one will guide us well, especially if we are new to praying, because it encompasses such broad themes: intimacy, worship, transformation, provision, grace and guidance.

Be careful. Prayer is more than saying the right words. Jesus debunked those who thought that eloquence or repetition would move God to act. Prayer is not some magic incantation by which we manipulate God (Matthew 6:7-8). No, prayer is honest, openhearted communication within a relationship of intimacy. Jesus comes alongside us in our journey and invites us to speak our minds and reveal our hearts. He wants to listen and he will respond out of his goodness and wisdom because he loves us.

Scripture

Jesus learned and lived by the Scriptures. He was a student of what we know as the Old Testament and understood those writings to be the Word of God. He also understood his own words to be the Word of God. Thus he prayed, "The words that you gave to me, I have given to them" (John 17:8). Furthermore, he made provision for what would be specially written after his departure, telling his inner circle, "When the Spirit of truth comes, he will guide you into all the truth, for he will not speak on his own, but will speak whatever he hears, and he will declare to you the things that are to come" (see John 16:12-15). Some of these core followers (such as Matthew, Peter and John) together with those they would directly influence (such as Mark, Luke and Paul) would compose the New Testament. From the beginning these Gospels and letters were collected and affirmed by the church as Scripture (see 2 Peter 3:15-16).

Perhaps Paul's declaration to young Timothy best captures why we as Christians immerse ourselves in the Scriptures:

> But as for you, continue in what you have learned and firmly believed, knowing from whom you learned it, and how from childhood you have known the sacred writings that are able to instruct you for salvation through faith in Christ Jesus. All scripture is inspired by God and is useful for teaching, for reproof, for correction, and for training in righteousness, so that everyone who belongs to God may be proficient, equipped for every good work. (2 Timothy 3:14-17)

First, *all Scripture is inspired by God*, that is, "God-breathed." In a mystery not unlike that of God taking on humanity in the incarnation, God breathes his Word into the words written by humans within their particular historical, cultural, linguistic and psychological contexts. In Scripture God speaks and reveals himself. Second, *all Scripture points toward Jesus* and the great salvation that he brings. The Scriptures contain good news, the gospel. They are words of life. Third, *all Scripture is useful* to teach and correct us, to train us for lives that please the Lord. They are words of truth that set us free to become the persons God created us to be. The Word of God is alive and powerful, able to transform us.

How then can we encounter the living God through these ancient Scriptures? There are many ways for the Biblical writings to be woven into our lives—sermons, teaching, memorization, singing, books—but I want to highlight two that are foundational, *study* and *meditation*.

Bible Study

Are you part of a group of people who meet to study the Bible? Perhaps a campus small group, a neighborhood Bible discussion, or a church cell group. Few things compare with the value and joy of studying the Scriptures in a small community of believers. We gain from each other's insights and help each other act on what we learn. We encounter the Lord together through his Word.

Invest in these five books and you'll have a great start for a lifelong Bible reference library:

How to Read the Bible for All Its Worth by Gordon Fee and Douglas Stuart, Zondervan.

The IVP Bible Background Commentary: New Testament by Craig Keener, InterVarsity Press.

The New Bible Atlas, InterVarsity Press.

The New Bible Commentary, 4th ed., InterVarsity Press.

The New Bible Dictionary, 3rd ed., InterVarsity Press.

Have you made time in your personal life for the study of Scripture? Perhaps a daily "quiet time" that includes Bible reading, a weekly hour or so of concentrated study or even classes on the Bible available at your church or nearby seminary? Lifelong study of the Word of God will move us ever deeper into relationship with God himself.

Bible Meditation

If Bible study is reading Scripture with an open mind, Bible *meditation* is reading it with an open heart. Here we cultivate a quiet spirit and a listening posture as we focus on a specific portion of Scripture. We do not analyze the text so much as absorb it. We turn it over in our thoughts, we let its words or images sink in. We may use our imagination to enter the text, especially narrative passages. We ponder the connections to our own experience. In short, we allow the Spirit to open the Scripture to us and us to the Scripture. This is a more intuitive approach, a valuable complement to rational study.

For many, this contemplative method allows them to hear God's voice in the words of Scripture more vividly. For example, a meditation on Luke 24 might lead you to consider such issues as where you are in your life journey, what disappointments or doubts lie in your heart, how Jesus might be present yet unrecognized in your life right now, or the power of the sacraments to convey the presence of Christ.

How can we connect with Jesus and experience his living presence? Where two or three gather in his name—to pray, to consider his Word, to break bread, to worship—he is always present.

Lord, open our eyes to see you.

Living Your Faith

1. How has Jesus been present in your recent experience? Could he be with you in some unrecognized way?

2. What is your personal communication with God like? Could Jesus' pattern of prayer be helpful to you?

3. Through which of the four means—prayer, Scripture, fellowship and worship—do you most readily connect with God? Which of these would you like to grow or strengthen in your life? What steps might you take to do that?

Recommended Reading

Drawing Close to God and *Quiet Time Dynamics* by Stephen Eyre, InterVarsity Press.

Prayer by Richard Foster, HarperCollins.

Praying the Scriptures by Evan Howard, InterVarsity Press.

Reading the Bible with Heart and Mind by Tremper Longman III, NavPress.

part two

Committed in
Relationships

"I believe in getting into hot water,
it keeps you clean."
G. K. CHESTERTON

"Courage is the ability to let go of
the familiar." Seen on a T-shirt

"Be extravagant for God or be extravagant
for the devil, but for God's sake, don't be tepid!"
C. T. STUDD

"Let love be genuine; hate what is evil, hold fast to
what is good; love one another with mutual affection;
outdo one another in showing honor. Do
not lag in zeal, be ardent in spirit, serve the Lord.
Rejoice in hope, be patient in suffering, persevere in
prayer. Contribute to the needs of the saints; extend
hospitality to strangers. . . .
Do not be overcome by evil, but overcome evil with good."
THE APOSTLE PAUL TO THE CHURCH IN ROME

six

Gambling on God
Jonathan Tran

I T WAS A COLD NIGHT DURING FINALS WEEK. ENRIQUE HAD MUCH to do and little time to do it. A twelve-page paper was due in History 110A the next morning. At 10:30 p.m. he was slightly ahead of schedule—he was on page one! While writing, a thought struck Enrique. *It's such a cold night in Riverside, I wonder how the homeless are dealing with this cold?* With his friend Jason, Enrique collected blankets and headed downtown. For the next hour, in the dark, in the worst parts of the city, during finals week, with papers due, the two college students handed out blankets to homeless men.

Jesus offers a life of risking. He interrupts our lives and asks, "Are you going to spend your life on your own glory, or do you want to live for something greater?" The preeminent temptation of our day is not some nefarious iniquity; it is the subtle, often silent, stroll into mediocrity. We spend an average of five hours a day in front of the television, looking for excitement from a two-dimensional made-up world, while letting life pass us by in the confined, three-dimensional world of our "living" rooms. Our greatest thrill of the day is reading the sports page; our deepest relationship is with some unknown cyber-friend we met two weeks ago on the Internet. We have traded in substantive dreams for those inspired by thirty-second commercials.

Into this world Jesus calls, "Come and I will make you fishers of people." He is offering us a life more exciting than anything imagined by the tinseled minds of Hollywood. He is calling us from our world of "settled arrangements," using Aladdin's words, to "a whole new world, a brand new place [you] never knew." He is offering us nothing less than the kingdom of God.

Betting the House

In the movie *Rounders* Matt Damon is a law-school student who earns his tuition by gambling. In the final scene of the movie we see him risking his very life on a high-stakes game in order to save a friend whose foolish gambling has endangered his own life. We wonder who would live this kind of life? Who would want to put it all on the line, to take such risks—the future always dependent on the next hand?

Christians do! We are the biggest gamblers on the planet. In following Jesus we bet the house. We risk our entire lives—our joy, our minds, our hearts—on God. We are betting that God exists, that he raised Jesus from the dead. Paul says that the gamble over the resurrection's truth will define us as either saints or the greatest fools in the history of fools. If the resurrection did not occur, he says, then we deserve the most pity of all creatures because we have gambled our whole lives on a bust (1 Corinthians 15:19).

We are gamblers for God. On this one hand we stake our entire lives. We are putting it all on the line, betting that God will come through for us. After we win that hand, we put down more on the next. We will not stop while we are ahead. The stakes keep on rising. We'll keep on betting until there is no more betting to be done. This *is* "faith on the edge."

Calling of the Gamblers

In Mark 1 we find two fishers, brothers Peter and Andrew, minding their own business, mending their nets. Fishing was no mere hobby but a means to survival. Further, it was their identity. It was the one thing they could do well. Jesus, an itinerant preacher from Nazareth, comes along. He approaches the two men. It is possible that the two men had either seen Jesus teaching and healing people or heard of his ministry, but there is no evidence that they had a significant relationship with him. "Follow me, and I will make you fish for people." An odd invitation! Why would they go with him? Especially right now, while they are working! *If you want to do that spiritual stuff, keep it for the sabbath; we're working right now!* they may have thought. *We can't just get up and leave our jobs! And what's it mean to be a fisher of people anyway? We're not into cannibalism.* Yet Mark 1:18 says, "Immediately they left their nets and followed him." Without hesitation they left their entire livelihoods to follow Jesus.

A short time later James and John, the "sons of thunder," are in their fishing boat with their father, Zebedee. Their closest friendship is with one another. The family is their primary set of relationships. All of a sudden Jesus comes along. Jesus "called them; and they left their father Zebedee in the boat with the hired men, and followed him" (Mark 1:20).

Peter and Andrew—gamblers. James and John—gamblers. They were willing to stake the two most important things in life, vocation/identity and relationships with family, on Jesus. They would trust a man they had never followed before. They were willing to "fish for people," whatever that meant. They did it for some small, tiny hope that this man Jesus was in fact the Messiah. They bet it all because they saw that the card showing was an ace and that their next card might be a king and that Jesus was going to use them to build his kingdom. They had nothing less than their vocations and family relationships on the line.

Peter, Andrew, James and John had no guarantees on how their lives would turn out. Jesus did not say, "If you follow me, I will make you fish for people, but if you don't catch anything, you can return to your lives as they were." Those four bet the house. If Jesus failed them, they would return to rotted nets and abandoned relationships.

The Only Guarantees That Count
There is much risk in the faithful Christian life. God *does* guarantee many

things in the Scriptures: joy, a loving relationship with him, his abiding presence, heaven, homes, brothers, sisters and his glory. However, we often seek guarantees in things that God is not offering, which ought to tell us that those things do not mean a whole lot to God. We look for guarantees in things like a 3.5 GPA (or better), a decent-paying job (*decent* is the code word for $60,000, or about one hundred times what the average earthling makes), peaceful relationships with our parents, a nice husband, a house in a cul-de-sac, eighty years on earth and good-looking, successful kids. God doesn't guarantee any of these. In fact, if you follow him faithfully, you may not have any of them.

John Piper, in a talk at Wheaton College, lamented how nearly every family that visited his inner-city ministry in Minneapolis asked, "Are my children going to be safe here?" God never guaranteed that our children would be safe. He says simply, "If you seek to save your life, you will lose it. If you lose your life for me and the gospel, you will save it" (see Mark 8:35). God guarantees that risking for him pays off in life. He also guarantees that risking to gain the whole world always pays off in "forfeiting your soul" (Mark 8:36).

When I entered college, my great dream was to go to law school. I wanted to be a United States Supreme Court Justice. I was sure I possessed the intellect, the drive and the plan. So I mapped out what I needed to do to get that appointment to the highest court in the land. I did well in school; I joined the prelaw societies, spent time learning from the successes and failures of other lawyers, and investigated law schools. In a constitutional law course, one of the hardest classes on campus, I was one of only two students who received an A. I thought, *If I can get one of only two As in Con Law 163, then certainly I can get one of only nine U.S. Supreme Court positions in the nation.* I was on my way.

Years passed as I worked toward my dream. Yet as I grew up in my relationship with Jesus, he introduced me to a whole new world, the world of loving God and neighbor. It was an entirely different world from Planet Jontran (my cosmology suggested a me-centric versus a heliocentric configuration of the planets and the stars). And I loved this new world. I loved how I looked at those around me. I loved that each day was an adventure with God: in learning to worship him and in the ways I served others. I began to sense that my life mattered. Though I did not sit on the Supreme Court, the decisions I made each day also had profound consequences. Though I would not go down in the annals of judiciary history, I was making kingdom history.

When graduation came around, I had a decision to make: law school or full-time staff with InterVarsity Christian Fellowship. Of course, law school promised a six-digit salary as well as a road to self-glory. InterVarsity staff promised a six-digit fundraising pincode and a road to college campuses where students desperately needed Jesus.

For me it was simple. Was I going to spend the next forty years of my life pursuing my dream and preparing my seat on the bench, or was I going to spend my life pursuing God's dream and preparing my seat before the throne? There are plenty of great things about being a lawyer, and there is no doubt that God calls some to the Supreme Court, but that was not God's plan for me. Becoming a lawyer was gaining the whole world yet forfeiting my soul. Instead, I want to spend my life risking, not being safe.

Jesus—Not Safe

I once saw a great "Christian" T-shirt. It pictured some classical painting of Christians being persecuted, while a large caption read, "Jesus—Not Safe." My life with Jesus has not been safe. I have had to risk much. In sacrificially serving others I risked being treated like a servant. In giving of myself to neighbors I risked losing my personal time and my favorite resources. By choosing a low-paying career I risked people not respecting me. In committing my life to the care of others in my community, I risked being hurt. And in the world's eyes I have risked and lost. I *have* been treated like a servant. I *have* lost my personal time and favorite resources. I *have* been incredibly disrespected, even by other Christians. I *have* been profoundly hurt by those in my community.

Yet in the kingdom's eyes, I've won the jackpot. Jesus comes through in the things he promised me. As I am treated like a servant, Jesus serves me. As I lose my personal time and favorite resources in seeking first his kingdom, he clothes me better than the lilies of the field and the birds of the air.

As the world looks at me with disrespect, Jesus calls me a child of the Most High God. Even as I am hurt by others in my community, he has died for those wounds.

Risking with Jesus means losing in the world's eyes yet winning in God's eyes. If you bet the whole house, you will gain all of Jesus. If you decide to play it safe in your faith-life, you may not get any of Jesus. He asks for high stakes. *At this blackjack table of the casino of God the minimum bet is your whole life.* If you want to bet any less, go do something boring and harmless like pursuing the American Dream.

Jesus: God of Gamblers

We are not the biggest gamblers; God is. He is the King of gamblers. Though we risk much by betting on Jesus, he risks much more by betting on us. It is a mystery why he bets on us, putting his kingdom in our hands, entrusting us with the precious things of his Word and choosing to find glory in serving us. Considering the human condition, this is absurd. Why bet on a sure loser? Jesus lost betting on us before. James, John and Peter, after betting the house by following Jesus, got into a big fight about which would be the greatest in the kingdom. Jesus bet the kingdom on them. Saul, who later became Paul, went around killing Christians. God bet the salvation of the Gentile world on him. Experienced gamblers say that you should leave a table if you lose several times straight. Well, according to this rule, God is a poor gambler. Yet he continues to bet on us.

God: A Really Good Bet

All things considered, placing it all on Jesus is a good bet. Amazingly, his glory is wrapped up in your winning. He wants you to win, and God knows how to win! He created life and has a good idea how to live it. Don't play it safe. Don't leave the table even though the risks look scary and the odds are stacked against you. Bet the whole house, you'll win it all.

Living Your Faith

1. How are you playing it safe right now, and what is God asking you to risk?

2. In what ways are you tempted to live a mediocre life?

3. When we gamble on God, we often lose in the world's eyes. For you, what have been some difficult losses?

How did Jesus come through for you even then?

4. What have been some "big hands" that you have won with Jesus?

Recommended Reading

A Long Obedience in the Same Direction by Eugene Peterson, InterVarsity Press.

My Utmost for His Highest by Oswald Chambers, Discovery House.

Upside-Down Kingdom by Bill Kraybill, Herald Press.

Wild Hope by Tom Sine, Word.

seven

Daring to Live
Life Together
Kevin Blue

ALL WHO BELIEVED WERE TOGETHER AND HAD ALL THINGS IN COMmon; they would sell their possessions and goods and distribute the proceeds to all, as any had need. Day by day, as they spent much time together in the temple, they broke bread at home and ate their food with glad and generous hearts, praising God and having the goodwill of all the people. And day by day the Lord added to their number those who were being saved" (Acts 2:44-47 RSV).

Notice the great unity among the believers in this text. In today's terms this sounds like a fellowship in which each member is married to all the others! All their possessions in some sense belong to everyone else. Any time there is a need, someone is willing to sell something to help meet it. They spend lots of time together, receive teaching from the apostles and enjoy meals in each others' homes. They are connected well enough to know the real needs in their fellowship. They share a rich life with many opportunities to learn and grow together.

This is not an event-oriented life in which they simply see people three times a week at Sunday worship, Wednesday night Bible study and prayer meeting on Thursday. They may come together for certain purposes like worship or prayer, but the depth of their relationships does not depend on these times. This unity and shared life is not forced on anyone, nor does it come out of concern for some cause. Earlier in Acts 2 we see that the people enter into community freely and gladly as part of their response of repentance which results in conversion. They are eager to give and receive the love of God. The Holy Spirit is active in their midst, and they respond to the lordship of Christ together. As this passage and others demonstrate, the evidence of being a believer is partly shown by our allegiance and commitment to other believers.

Life Together

The message of Acts 2:44-47 may fall hard on our ears today. It strikes a deathblow to any sense of radical individualism and independence. So often I hear people say, "I believe," but they are not committed to any gathering of believers. The Word of God and the model of Jesus and the apostles simply do not give us this option. In fact, Hebrews 10:24-25 tells us directly not to neglect meeting together.

I understand that the institutional or formal church has let many of us down. Though I too have been disappointed at times by the poor quality of teaching and the insincerity of relationships in various churches, I must continue to walk in my commitment. I too have failed people, taught poorly and been insincere. But Jesus calls us to bear with one another through these things, to love one another as he loved us (John 13:34). We must therefore commit ourselves to being a part of some type of Christian fellowship.

Think of it like this. When we pledge ourselves in faith to Christ, several things happen. We receive forgiveness for our sins (Jesus as our Savior), and we begin to follow him as disciples (Jesus as our Lord). We also pledge ourselves to one another. These are inseparable truths. If we have not fully embraced them, we have misunderstood the nature of the gospel.

In marriage two people pledge to be united and to love each other whether they are sick or well, rich or poor, regardless of what kind of person each turns out to be. When I provide premarital counseling, I usually try to help people connect with these realities by posing certain scenarios. I often ask, "Will you be committed to her and love her for the remainder of your life if the day after your wedding she is struck by a car and becomes a paraplegic? Will you continue to be a devoted wife and care for him if he contracts Alzheimer's disease and cannot even remember your name?" Such are the pledges of marriage, which we take lightly at times.

When we become Christians, we similarly pledge ourselves to God and to each other in this fashion. Yet so often I hear people make excuses: "Well, our congregation is suffering from a great deal of gossip now; the relationships seem superficial, and the new pastor's teaching is not very good."

It's easy to love when your partner is strong, beautiful and wealthy. Virtually anyone would at least try to be committed under the most favorable circumstances. But the love of Christ is sacrificial and doesn't walk out regardless of the struggles of the other. It loves despite sickness, poverty and conflict. Love that is this pure, strong and enduring only comes as a fruit of the Spirit's work in us (Galatians 5:22).

There are at least four elements that help make an "Acts 2 community" a reality: being real, discipline, decision-making, and open doors for outsiders to enter.

Being Real

We must be specific when we share how we're doing or what we need to confess, where we need encouragement or what we are currently facing in our lives. Our words with one another should be highly valued and not simply cast about. I am privileged to have been a part of fellowships where people confessed specific sin openly. No one was shocked to hear it or mocked for saying it. People did not run out and gossip about it. Rather they prayed for that brother or sister. They worked to recognize the dignity, the struggle and the humanity of the person and rightly stood in awe of how God helped them confess their sin. Though I have been glad to witness some physical healings, I find far more precious the healing of "wounds" caused by our own sin or the sin of others against us. Being real is a challenge, but it is necessary if trust, deep relationships and the simple grace of God are to grow among us.

Necessary Discipline

When a person falls into sin, some form of accountability and encouragement is necessary. Once when I had lied, I became aware of it and told my prayer partner. We prayed about it, asking and thanking the Lord for his forgiveness (1 John 1:9). But then I needed to finish the work of repentance by telling the truth to the person I lied to and asking forgiveness. That was harder than simply praying about it or talking it over in secret with a trusted friend. It took greater courage and was far more humbling. My lie was about a stupid thing and was committed for no other reason than I wanted to be seen in a particular way. My prayer partner walked me through the restoration process by praying for me over the next few days as I tried to get together with the person I lied to. Later he asked me about it to be sure I had done it and to see how it went. Though this is a relatively minor example, sin is sin. It all needs to be taken seriously. Being in Christian community means we are willing to love each other by challenging one another and giving and receiving the necessary discipline in each other's lives.

Decision Making

Another important element of a rich community life is the giving and receiving of wisdom. A powerful expression of this comes in submitting life decisions to the counsel of others in the community. Scripture strongly encourages this among believers. Each person must own their decisions, for they are accountable to God for them. But they should recognize that God's direction also comes through others. Paul develops this concept in 1 Corinthians 12, describing the community of believers as a human body.

Just as parts of the human body are dependent on each other, each person's life decisions affect the lives of other members of the group. As we learn to trust each other to give and receive counsel, God frequently gives wisdom to us through fellow believers. This is central to a vibrant fellowship. We must make decisions and go through life together: each caring for the sorrows of the others and celebrating their joys (Romans 12:15), and each sharing in the burdens and responsibilities of others (Galatians 6:2).

Cori and Chris were each recovering from some difficult issues involved in their dating relationships with other people. Each sought and received valuable counsel from a couple of friends and a pastoral leader regarding their relationships with the opposite sex. They each accepted that wise counsel and decided not to date anyone, focusing instead on forming quality friendships with the opposite sex. Cori and Chris began building this type of relationship with several people, including each other. Early on, however, they were attracted to each other and felt drawn into old patterns of romantic relating. But they decided to pray and discuss this with those who previously had helped them work through these issues. They were reminded that the Lord's wisdom for them is not to go with their sensual urges but to become good, strong friends, holding to their original commitment.

Cori and Chris's faithfulness in relating to one another, and their willingness, even eagerness, to seek and listen to the wise counsel of others at all stages of their relationship, has been a strong witness and a great encouragement to many. This kind of community decision-making involves choosing to have one's life entwined with and affected by the lives of others.

Dating is a very sensitive area of decision-making for most people. Communal wisdom is useful not only in making major or sensitive decisions but in more ordinary situations as well. We need to encourage and exhort one another in the faith. Many fellowships and churches have small groups for this purpose, gathering together for confession of sin, prayer and encouragement. Small group discussion and prayer have proven extremely valuable to me in sharpening my sense of how God has gifted me and how to develop those gifts, discovering and recovering from areas of weakness, overcoming patterns of sin, and deciding which course of life to take.

Finally, we should not just seek counsel from those who will tell us only what we *want* to hear. We need people who will tell us what we *need* to hear and who will take this role seriously. They cannot simply be a committee to rubber stamp whatever it is we want to do.

Open Doors

The internal dynamics of community relationships and those of outreach are intricately woven together. As he prayed for his disciples, Jesus offered these words to the Father: "I ask not only on behalf of these [my disciples], but also on behalf of those who will believe in me through their word, that they may all be one. As you, Father, are in me and I am in you, may they also be in us, *so that the world may believe that you have sent me*" (John 17:20-21, emphasis added).

Our unity sends a clear, authenticating message to the world of Jesus' credentials as the Messiah. Plenty of people discuss amazing ideas, but witnessing a fellowship that exhibits the love of God in this tangible way could be quite convicting for a seeker or even an atheist.

Shawn entered college as a committed atheist. He even enjoyed discouraging Christians and making them doubt their faith. On a hot afternoon several fellowship members offered to help Shawn and his mom move things into the dorm. Even though he was parked blocks away, he was not used to receiving help, so he turned them down. After another trip he and his mom had a good sweat going and, fairly exhausted, he broke down and agreed to receive help. In a few minutes several fellowship members were rounded up and the rest of Shawn's belongings were brought up in one trip. Sweating, tired and thankful (though a bit uncomfortable), Shawn went to the room across the hall to thank the guys for their help. He noticed that the refrigerator was full of soda (the guys had stocked it to serve folks on a hot day). When he was offered a couple of sodas, Shawn decided he could not impose by taking two. He took only one to split with his mom and returned to his room.

Days later he was invited to the first fellowship meeting of the year. Though he had no interest in going, he felt obligated because of the soda, so he went. He hated the meeting and swore he would never attend anything else this group sponsored. Over the next couple of weeks Shawn was well served by the upperclassmen in the Christian fellowship. Through them he met a lot of people on campus. He did some fun things with them that helped make the transition into college easier. The guys also invited him to the first Bible study they were having in their room. Firm in his resolve, he told them he wouldn't like it. Not to be put off so easily, one of the upperclassmen responded, "How do you know you wouldn't like it if you've never been to a Bible study?" Shawn couldn't really argue with that so he went just to prove his point.

They studied the prodigal son story from Luke 15, and the discussion was lively. Though he disagreed with the way they understood the passage (he thought it was a great example of bad parenting), he liked the people and enjoyed the discussion. He gradually became a regular. Over time he found himself liking Jesus and began to think about God when he wasn't with his friends. As you can imagine, this was fairly disturbing for an atheist. God was drawing Shawn to himself through the way these guys loved each other and loved him. It was their sacrificial service and love that God used to present the gospel in action and to prepare Shawn's heart to receive the good news of Jesus' love for him.

Three months after school started the avowed atheist walked into the kingdom as a new believer. The authentic Christian fellowship of this community was a powerful witness to Shawn. The result was a life saved from the ravages and penalty of sin.

The Struggle with Our Culture

A thriving, local faith fellowship in our age of fast food, rapid transit and ever quicker telecommunications is hard to come by because it costs us some things we find very precious. Speed and efficiency are values that seep into nearly every facet of life. But the formation of authentic Christian fellowship requires time. This rich and beautiful life comes gradually. It is not a common kind of life in our world today, and for this reason Christian community will always be prophetic in our society. But such truth and beauty, richness and wisdom, empowerment, resilience and cleansing power of community await those of us who would dare to be different and live out the kind of challenging and fulfilling life that God offers to us—together.

Living Your Faith

1. Of the four elements of community life (being real, discipline, decision-making and open doors for outsiders), which do you find most personally challenging?

2. Which of the four is the least present in your fellowship? How might

it become more of a reality? Where will you take your next steps forward?

3. It is difficult to take advice from others about issues that are very personal. Cori and Chris sought out counsel when their attraction for each other developed; would you likewise seek out and submit to the counsel of wise friends? Should this be a role Christian community plays in the lives of its members?

Recommended Reading

Beyond Charity by John Perkins, Baker.

Life Together by Dietrich Bonhoeffer, Harper & Row.

eight

Learning to Love
the Church
Bobby Gross

I GREW UP IN THE CHURCH—THE FIRST BAPTIST CHURCH OF COLUM-
bus, Georgia, to be exact. It was one of five prominent churches
downtown that leading citizens and well-to-do families attended.
This was to be expected in the Bible belt of the fifties and sixties. The
members were all white. This too was to be expected, back then. The 11:00
a.m. service in our stately sanctuary, complete with magnificent organ, was
televised live on a local channel. The service always lasted exactly sixty
minutes. And it always ended with an invitation to come forward to accept
Jesus as personal Lord and Savior.

As far back as I can remember, I went to Sunday school. At age eight I
was baptized (dunked, of course). Later I sang in the youth choir. During
my teens, several men and women invested in me as a young Christian and
had a strong impact on my life and faith. By the time I left for college, I
was a solid follower of Jesus and eager to continue my growth.

In my first week at the University of North Carolina, I discovered Inter-
Varsity and plunged in enthusiastically. Our chapter meetings hummed

with energy: spirited singing, upbeat testimonies and challenging speakers. I immediately joined an "action group" that met weekly in my dorm for Bible study, prayer and fellowship. I formed Christian friendships right and left. Spiritually, I entered a tremendous growth phase.

During my first Sundays in Chapel Hill, I naturally donned my coat and tie and attended the Baptist church. It paralleled my home church exactly: sixty minutes, three hymns, two anthems and one sermon with an invitation. Suddenly, "church" seemed staid compared to the campus fellowship. Why couldn't it be dynamic in the same way? Then I heard about a church that drew many students. I visited one Sunday and left amazed.

Chapel Hill Bible Church, independent, nondenominational and only a few years old, met on campus in a small auditorium. Everyone dressed casually. They sang praise songs accompanied by guitars. Opportunity was given for anyone to stand and share how God was at work in his or her life. At prayer time, anyone could pray aloud. The pastor taught from a passage of Scripture, showing his outline on an overhead projector. The energy and vision of that congregation were palpable. Furthermore, the church leaders enthusiastically endorsed our involvement in campus fellowships, seeing us as missionaries to the university. Not surprisingly, I stayed on.

Surely this must be closer to what the New Testament church was like— open, spontaneous and Spirit-led, I thought. Quickly, I developed a critical attitude toward my former church with its buildings, formality and traditionalism. Later when I shared my discoveries with my home pastor, he lacked my enthusiasm (only proving my point, I thought at the time). Years later, my perspectives recalibrated, I realized that the Bible church had its share of flaws and drawbacks. I also began to see that the Lord had been present and active at First Baptist—after all, that's where I first embraced and began to follow Jesus.

What has been your experience of "church"? Did you grow up attending a church? Are your memories positive or negative? What kind of church are you part of now? Are you satisfied or dissatisfied? These lead to other questions. How do we choose which church to join in the first place? And once we are part of one, what should be our expectations and involvement? Finally, underlying all of these, what is God's purpose for the church in the world?

The New Testament Church

Two thousand years ago Jesus appeared on the Galilean scene proclaiming the presence of the kingdom of God. And he backed up his preaching with action: he healed the diseased, exorcised demons, multiplied food, calmed storms and loved the poor. Jesus called people to believe the good news and follow him. Those who did gradually came to understand, as Simon Peter once exclaimed, that Jesus was "the Messiah [or Christ], the son of the living God." To which Jesus replied, "I tell you, you are Peter, and on this rock I will build my church, and the gates of Hades will not prevail against it" (see Matthew 16:13-20).

Did Jesus intend to found the church as we know it? Yes and no. No, in that Jesus did not give a blueprint for structures of church government or liturgies for weekly worship or strategies for running a stewardship campaign. Yes, in that Jesus did lay the groundwork for a community of men and women centered on himself as the Christ, sharing together in his life and working together in his mission. We don't get the structural details from Jesus—he knew these would develop over time—but we do get the essential values that should mark the community bearing his name.

Here are a few of the things Jesus emphasized to his followers during his intimate conversation with them the night before he was killed (see John 13—17).

□ We are to *love one another as he has loved us,* demonstrated in the kind of humble service that Jesus modeled when he washed the grimy feet of his friends (John 13).

□ We are to *be a "home" for the Holy Spirit,* who is the very presence of Jesus and the Father, the Advocate who guides and guards us, the Spirit of truth (John 14).

□ We are to *stay vitally connected to the life and love of Jesus,* like branches to vine and trunk, so as to produce fruit that honors God and draws attention to him (John 15).

□ We are to *pursue a profound unity* so that the people around us would know that Jesus was sent into the world in love and that we are his beloved and joy-filled followers (John 17).

Weaving just these few threads together, we see the church as the community of those who are united in the Father's love, indwelt by the Holy Spirit, marked by Christlikeness and bearing witness to the watching world.

Reading the rest of the New Testament only enriches our understanding. In Acts 2 the community of Christ-followers entered a new phase of life together; filled with the promised Holy Spirit and united around the Word of God; the communal, eucharistic meals; and the practice of prayer. A joyous energy filled them, daily attracting new believers.

Rich metaphors describe the church: the *body of Christ* (1 Corinthians 12), the *bride of Christ* being cleansed and adorned (Ephesians 5), a *spiritual house* built on the Living Cornerstone (1 Peter 2), to name a few. Furthermore, these writers make it clear that in this new community there is no room for "isms": racism, classicism, sexism, favoritism, legalism or egotism. Rather, we are to practice the "one another" principle, that is, to show one another compassion, kindness, humility, meekness, patience, forbearance and forgiveness. In short, we are to love one another (see Colossians 3).

But if that's what the church is supposed to be like, then what is this that I'm in? you may be thinking.

Before you despair of finding a church like the above or decide in frustration to bail out of where you are, remember two important truths: *we are sinners* and *God is gracious.* A reminder of our sinfulness comes in this familiar quip: if you ever find the perfect church, don't join it—it would no longer be perfect. The truth is, there is no perfect church. Read the New Testament carefully and you will discover the underside of the tapestry: disciples arguing over who was the greatest (Luke 22:24-27), workers distributing food with an ethnic bias (Acts 6:1-6), believers getting drunk at the Lord's Supper (1 Corinthians 11:20-22), worshipers boasting of their spiritual gifts (1 Corinthians 12—14), leaders teaching false doctrines (2 Timothy 3:1-9) and Christians discriminating against the poor (James 2:1-7). Still, God was present and active, carrying forward his purposes despite human flaws and sinfulness. The same is true today. So we should not be too quick to pass judgment. We *do* need discernment, however, when initially choosing a church.

Choosing a Church

Churches vary considerably in character and quality. When we find ourselves in transition and needing to choose a new church, I would *not* recommend simply looking up the nearest congregation in the yellow pages. We need to choose with care. After all, we are not simply signing up for a place that offers weekly programs, like a local health club where we'll work out twice a week. Rather, we are joining our lives with others in a spiritual community.

After college I moved to Gainesville, home of the University of Florida. Here's what I looked for in a church: dynamic worship, strong biblical preaching, small groups or some similar avenue for meaningful relationships, and interest in student ministry. I found all but the lively worship at Community Evangelical Free Church. I was quite pleased.

But then, over the next few years, Jesus opened new chapters in my journey with him. I began to wrestle with two major issues, materialism and racism, grappling not only with the reality of these sins in my own life and in society but also with the biblical mandates to seek social justice and pursue racial reconciliation. As a step of obedience and a means of broadening my experience and understanding, I decided to visit a black church near my home.

I arrived at Williams Temple Church of God in Christ one Sunday morning promptly at 10:50 a.m. (As it turned out, the service would not start for another half-hour.) I was the only white person present, and I was most warmly welcomed. The service was like none I had ever been in, a surprising mixture of dignified formality and spirited spontaneity. The congregation sang and clapped with vigor, testified with great emotion and responded to the choir and preacher with verbal enthusiasm. I must admit, sheepishly, that after two hours I left with a headache, the end of the service nowhere in sight. My first Pentecostal church experience! But I came back, attending every few weeks over several years. I puzzled deeply over these two churches. Same God, same Bible, same faith, but such different expressions of worship and outreach. For example, at Williams Temple I found emotional engagement and concern for the poor; at Community, intellectual stimulation and vision for world missions. What I gained from the one, I missed at the other. Thankfully, my life as a Christian was shaped by both.

By the time I moved to Miami with my wife, whose own primary—and positive—church experience was Roman Catholic, our joint list of criteria had expanded to include multiethnic membership, Spirit-inspired vitality, concern for social justice and emphasis on lay leadership. We visited half a dozen churches before settling on a charismatic Episcopal church. For the first time, I was worshiping in a liturgical and sacramental context. At first I was bewildered by the standing and kneeling, the crosses and candles, the collects and choral responses, the prayer book and lectionary, and the wafers and (real) wine. Over time, however, I came to deeply appreciate and enjoy this rich tradition. C. S. Lewis once remarked that learning the liturgy is like learning to dance, the enjoyment only comes when you are able to focus on your partner rather than thinking about the steps.

I share my own "church journey" because it illustrates several important considerations. First, the church in its broadest, universal sense is composed of an amazing diversity of denominations and congregations, reflecting the amazing complexity of our God. Do not be too quick to dismiss the churches in your own tradition, nor those unfamiliar to you in another tradition. Second, when considering a potential church, participate long enough to really get to know it before you make your decision; include exposure to the congregation's life beyond Sunday worship and conversations with the leaders. Third, accept that you probably won't find one church that satisfies all your desires. This may be especially true if you've recently graduated from college and have enjoyed a tightly knit, mission-driven, student-led campus fellowship. It's not wise to expect a church to duplicate that experience. Rather, think about what fresh elements you will gain in your new community and how you can positively contribute from your campus ministry or other previous experience.

Being Part of a Church

Once you—or perhaps a small group of you—have done your homework and prayerfully chosen a church, it is time to shift from a questioning posture to a commitment posture. Belonging to a Christian community should not be a marginal element of our lives but a central priority. The following simple guidelines can lead to more satisfying and fruitful participation.

Give it time. Determine to stay involved for several years in a wholehearted way. Resist the temptation to leave after your first disappointment.

Don't be a fickle consumer, ready to switch brands whenever an exciting new preacher comes to First Church or an appealing new program is launched at Second Tabernacle. Don't even assume that an offer of promotion and job transfer is automatically God's will; sometimes our commitment to our Christian community will take priority.

Build relationships. Take the initiative to get to know people and be willing to invest in budding friendships. If your church offers small groups of any sort, join one. The heart of community is likely to be found there. If your church doesn't have small groups, explore with your pastor the idea of starting one. Be sure to seek out a few relationships with some who are different from you—if you are twentysomething, perhaps with an older person; if you are single, perhaps with a married couple or a family; if you are an artist, perhaps with a businessperson.

Get involved. In Gainesville I first volunteered to teach third grade Sunday school. In Miami my first role was usher; when we moved to New York, nursery worker. Volunteer to serve, even if your first opportunity doesn't utilize your strongest gifts. In time those who get involved with a serving attitude will be asked to take on more significant roles in keeping with their gifts and passions. In Gainesville I eventually taught adult education, in Miami I became a home-group leader, and now I serve as Senior Warden (you'll have to look it up!).

Support the leadership. Pastors have a tough job. Every week they face a demanding range of needs and expectations. Often we are unaware of the weight they carry: parishioners whose marriages are on the verge of collapse, who are battling dark sins or deep emotional needs, who are experiencing grief or facing death. Add to this the barrage of criticism and complaint that many endure. We need, therefore, to come alongside our pastors, not with both barrels loaded but with words of encouragement and pledges to pray. Let him or her find in you an ally, not another weight added to the burden.

Vision for the Church

Jesus continues to build his church in the world. You will find expressions of it in virtually every nation, every culture, every city. Graciously he builds it out of ordinary, sinful people, men and women who have embraced him as the Christ, the Son of the living God. And while we are not competent in ourselves, he makes us competent by his presence in and among us. He forms us into loving communities that bear witness to him by words and actions. Out of great gratitude and love for him we give ourselves to one another and together to his purposes in the world.

I am now part of All Angels' (Episcopal) Church on the Upper West Side of Manhattan. Twenty years ago a tiny remnant of a congregation sold its historic, cathedral-like building and moved into the narrow, four-story parish house. They called a visionary priest, and she came and preached the gospel afresh. God began to rebuild the church, not a stately building but a spiritual community. We learned to infuse the liturgy with heartfelt worship. We experienced the power of God to heal. We reached out to the poor and homeless. We welcomed everyone, from Wall Street bankers to aspiring artists. We grew. Now several pastors later, having weathered our share of setbacks, we remain an amazingly diverse congregation growing in love and in a profound sense of mission: *to build Christ-centered communities of witness and healing and to equip people to be a transforming presence in New York City and beyond.* This is worth the investment of my life. This is the church, a community of the King in the midst of a needy world. And the gates of hell will not stand against it!

Living Your Faith

1. If you grew up attending church, what three things do you most appreciate about your home church?

2. In your current church, what do you gain? What do you give?

3. What is your church's mission? Are you able to embrace that mission?

4. Do you share with others a vision for your church?

Recommended Reading

Church: Why Bother? by Philip Yancey, Zondervan.

The Community of the King by Howard Snyder, InterVarsity Press.

Truly the Community: Romans 12 and How to Be the Church by Marva J. Dawn, Eerdmans.

nine

Risking Forgiveness
Amy Brooke

I LIED TO KARA AND THEN LIED TO COVER UP MY LIE. EVERY TIME
that it mushroomed into another lie, I felt guilty. However, my fear
that the relationship would end if I confessed outweighed the guilt.

Kara too was conscious of the fragility of our relationship. As a result
she only hinted at her suspicions. After a year of uncertainty she called the
relationship and me into truth.

The day Kara confronted me, it took everything in me not to run away
but to stay and answer her questions truthfully. It took several conversations to sort out what was true and what wasn't and where we should go
from there. I cried for the pain I had caused and from the fear that it meant
the relationship would end.

I could have easily chosen never to see her again instead of working
through the situation. Similarly, Kara could have chosen to wash her hands
of me. Because we chose to work through it, our relationship is now more
secure than ever.

Jesus valued us enough to die to see us forgiven and reconciled to God.

Thus forgiveness and reconciliation are part of what it means to follow him. Understanding God's desire to see us forgive one another, and the conviction of the value of the relationship and the people involved, drive us forward in forgiving or allowing ourselves to be forgiven when running away would be infinitely easier.

What Is Forgiveness?

"Forgive and forget."

"Turn the other cheek."

"Say you're sorry and move on."

While each of these ideas has some validity, they often don't tell the whole story of forgiveness and leave us wondering if anyone can ever truly forgive. What happens when I say I forgive another person but I know I can't forget? Am I really expected to invite more pain? What if "I'm sorry" just doesn't seem to cut it?

Forgiveness takes time. *We need to understand that forgiveness is a process.* The deeper the wound, the longer the process.

There is a story about a woman who told a priest that she had a prophecy for him. The priest agreed to listen if God told the woman his sins. A week later the woman told him that God had answered. "What did he say?" asked the astonished priest. The woman smiled. "He said he didn't remember."

It is a clever but inaccurate story. God remembers our sin. Scripture says that we will have to give an account for everything we do and say (Matthew 12:36-37; Romans 14:10-12; 2 Corinthians 5:10; Hebrews 4:12-13). The idea of God forgetting our sin is a metaphor for the fact that if we are Christians, he will no longer hold us accountable. How much more amazing that makes the idea of God's forgiveness! God knows all of our failures and still chooses to forgive!

Likewise, it may be impossible for us to "forget" the harm another has done us. Forgiveness means we choose to hold another blameless even though the hurt and anger may resurface at times. We revoke the right to avenge the wrong done to us even though we remember it. *Forgiveness does not mean automatically forgetting.*

The danger in talking about forgetting is in pretending it doesn't matter.

When we pretend a wrong doesn't matter, we risk belittling the injuries of the wounded party. Even though Frank is deeply remorseful for causing Tim to break his leg and Tim has forgiven him, Tim still feels the pain of the leg. The same is true of emotional pain. *True forgiveness does not negate the pain and the mending that needs to happen.* The pain must be dealt with honestly. Pretending that it doesn't matter obscures reality and may cause further injury.

If the church treasurer repents for embezzlement, the church may help him find other ways of serving. Forgiveness doesn't mean patting him on the back and allowing him to continue as treasurer. The church leaders will require him to pay back what he stole, receive counseling and have an "accountability partner" who will meet with him regularly. He is forgiven, but a consequence of his sin is that trust was broken. Eventually it may be regained, but it takes time. *Forgiveness needs to be handled in a way that maintains the integrity and humanity of all involved.*

Forgiveness on an emotional level is similar. If Sherry continually insults Lisa and asks for forgiveness but then does it *again and again*, Lisa needs to set a boundary. She can warn Sherry that she will leave at the first insult and then follow through. Is this not forgiving? Lisa is actually acting more lovingly than if she allows Sherry to continue to abuse her in the name of forgiveness.

In my situation with Kara, forgiveness had a price: the knowledge that I had hurt Kara, the shame of what I had done and some pride. It meant being willing to go back over all of the lies and admit them, apologizing and shedding a lot of tears. It meant being determined to change and taking an honest look at who I am and my ability to sin. Worse yet, it meant letting Kara see all of that as well.

It cost Kara by putting the security of the relationship on the line. She also had to go through the process of figuring out what was true and what wasn't and dealing with any feelings my lies had brought up for her. She revoked a right for revenge—the desire to hurt me the way I hurt her. *The strange thing about forgiveness is that it costs both the offended and the offender.*

A Bible Study on Forgiveness

"You have heard that it was said to those of ancient times, 'You shall not murder'; and 'whoever murders shall be liable to judgment.' But I say to you that if you are angry with a brother or sister, you will be liable to judgment; and if you insult a brother or sister, you will be liable to the council; and if you say, 'You fool,' you will be liable to the hell of fire. So when you are offering your gift at the altar, if you remember that your brother or sister has something against you, leave your gift there before the altar and go; first be reconciled to your brother or sister, and then come and offer your gift" (Matthew 5:21-24).

"If another member of the church sins against you, go and point out the fault when the two of you are alone. If the member listens to you, you have regained that one" (Matthew 18:15).

1. Read Matthew 5:21-24. What is the situation?

2. How might anger toward another person interfere with a person's relationship to God?

3. Read Matthew 18:15. How should a disagreement first be handled? Why?

4. What is the potential benefit of working through the situation?

5. Look at both passages. Who is responsible in each passage for forgiveness and reconciliation?

How might this insight affect the way you deal with conflict?

Myron's comments had infuriated me. As we sat in worship at the conference, I fumed. And then I thought about the unkind things I had said. As I prayed, God convicted me of my responsibility in the situation. As soon as possible I went to find Myron.

I ran into him coming out of the camp lodge. "I was looking for you," we both blurted out. God had brought us both under the conviction that we needed to talk things out.

Scripture tells us that when it comes to forgiveness, we are never off the hook. *Forgiveness is the responsibility of both parties.* If we need to forgive someone, we are responsible to go to them. If we have offended someone (or even suspect that we have), we need to go to them. As I found out with Myron, it is a joy to meet in the middle—seeking to forgive and be forgiven—and it is obedience to Scripture. However, if we don't "meet in the middle," we—the offender or the offended—must initiate the process of forgiveness. Why? Because God's Word tells redeemed, forgiven people that we must.

Why Should We Forgive?

The best reason for forgiving is that God has forgiven us. Matthew 18:23-35 records Jesus telling the story of a slave who owed his master more than he could pay in his lifetime. When he asked his master for more time, the master went *beyond the request* and canceled the debt. Later, the slave ran into a man who owed him a very small amount of money. Because the man couldn't pay, the slave had him thrown into jail. When the master found out, he said, "Should you not have had mercy on your fellow slave, as I had mercy on you?" (Matthew 18:33). He had the slave handed over to the authorities until he could pay the entire debt. By refusing to forgive, the slave cut himself off from the master's grace and forgiveness.

As forgiven people we are responsible to forgive. When we fail to forgive or at least begin the process of forgiving, like the slave we risk cutting ourselves off from experiencing God's grace.

A Snapshot of God's Forgiveness

A Christian's life is to be patterned after Jesus. Therefore, before talking about our process of forgiveness, we must understand God's process of forgiveness.

In the book of Hosea God instructs the prophet Hosea to take a wife. At first Gomer is content in marriage. She bears Hosea a son, but then Gomer's eyes begin to wander, and she then bears two children who aren't Hosea's.

Gomer has become an adulteress, but then she takes it one step further and begins to sell herself. When I read this story, I grieve for Hosea and the pain this experience must have caused him. I expect him to wash his hands of her, but then God does the unthinkable. He tells Hosea to go and find Gomer, to buy her out of prostitution and to love her as the Lord loves Israel. The only catch is that Gomer must give up prostitution and adultery.

God brought the Israelites out of Egypt and entered into a covenant with them. He would be their God and they would be his people. Over and over in the Old Testament we see the Israelites running after other gods. But the Lord God is determined to bring his people back into relationship with him even though it may cost him dearly.

Scripture shows us several things about God's forgiveness:

☐ *All people belong to God.* God created us and has a creational right to us. He desires to be in a covenant (marriage-like) relationship with us.

☐ *We break the covenant.* Like Gomer we prostitute ourselves for our own immediate profit or pleasure by making other things more important than God through our actions or attitudes. Sin breaks the covenant just as adultery breaks marriage vows.

☐ *God is angry and grieved by our sin.* Hosea 2:2-13 is about God's anger and sadness over Israel's unfaithfulness and ours. The opposite of love isn't anger or hate but apathy. God loves us enough not to be apathetic about sin!

☐ *God determines to forgive us even at a cost.* Through marriage Gomer already belonged to Hosea, but he paid fifteen shekels of silver and a homer and a lethek of barley for her. By buying her back, he offered forgiveness.

When we sin, we become slaves to sin. A payment must be made to set us free. To pay for the sin we committed, Jesus died on the cross. Our sin cost God his only son. In Jesus' death, God offers all of us forgiveness.

☐ *Reconciliation costs us.* Hosea's offer of forgiveness was costly to him, but it was free to Gomer. Hosea's paying of Gomer's debt freed her from being sold as a slave but didn't guarantee her relationship with Hosea. To be reconciled with Hosea, Gomer needed to give up prostitution and adultery to renew the relationship with Hosea. In biblical terms she needed to repent—to turn and go the other way.

The cost is the same for us. God's offer of ultimate forgiveness comes at a cost to himself. The cost of reconciliation falls on our ability to accept that the debt has been paid, admit what we have done and determine to go the other way.

The Process of Forgiveness

A woman I know was molested by a relative from the time she was a child until she was a teenager. She feels like the abuse permeates every fiber of her being in the way she relates to people, in her depression and in her self-destructive behavior. How is she supposed to forgive?

In spite of the damage, God does want her to forgive. In forgiving she frees herself from being consumed by anger and the desire for revenge. When she forgives, she puts everything in God's hands. It requires immense courage to go through the process of forgiving, but in doing so she frees herself from a life trapped by rage.

God wants us to forgive the horrendous acts that are committed against us. Jesus prayed that God would forgive those who crucified him. *Sometimes the first step is to ask God, "Make me willing to forgive."*

Our process of forgiveness goes along similar lines. Just as it cost God, it will cost us.

1. Look honestly at the damage. The risk of not taking stock of the injury is to forgive prematurely. Both parties need to acknowledge the harm that has been done.

2. Feel the pain and anger. Emotions are tricky things. We can sit on them for a time, but they usually leak out (sometimes explode) later. Owning the feelings eventually frees us up to fully forgive.

3. Determine to release the offender. Having worked through the feelings, the injured party needs to emotionally release the offender, even an unrepentant offender. By holding on to the anger and hurt, the offended (not the offender) is held captive by the situation. In releasing the offender the offended revokes the right for revenge and is freed up to renew the relationship and to live a happier life. Being angry is costly in time and energy.

When I refuse to forgive, my heart's responsiveness to God hardens. Like the unforgiving slave I cut myself off from God's grace. I must weigh which is more important: (a) my anger at the wrong done to me or (b) the vitality of my relationship with God.

4. The parties must clear the air. Voicing the hurt and ultimately the forgiveness allows the offended to solidify the commitment to forgive and move forward. It gives the offender the opportunity to repent.

5. Reconciliation happens when there is repentance and a determination to change. This step falls primarily to the offender. Without a willingness on the part of the offender to change, the injured party is open to continual injury by staying in the relationship. The offender needs to own the damage caused and work toward not doing it again. Only then can the relationship be fully healed.

At any point one or more of these things may be happening. The extent of the injury will determine the time the process takes.

Forgiveness is rarely as easy as saying your sorry. However, on the other side of the hard work of forgiveness and reconciliation is the joy of restored relationship.

Living Your Faith

1. How might you need to change your way of thinking about forgiveness?

How might this make a difference in your life?

2. What did you find surprising about God's forgiveness?

What difference does it make to you that it is like that?

3. Which part of the process of forgiveness do you think would be the most difficult for you? Why?

4. Is there someone who has sinned against you that you need to forgive?

5. Is there someone you have sinned against that you need to confess your sins to and seek reconciliation?

Recommended Reading

Bold Love by Dan Allender and Tremper Longman III, NavPress.
Forgive and Forget by Lewis B. Smedes, HarperSanFrancisco.
The Wounded Heart by Dan Allender, NavPress.

ten

Racial Reconciliation

Kevin Blue

F— YOU, NIGGER."
Hearing this comment from a stranger driving by me as I put a letter in the mailbox was tough. Not that I haven't heard these words before, but this seemed particularly aggressive.

Problems with race relations have been a central concern in the United States since well before the founding of the country. Slavery, race riots, separate-but-equal legislation and institutional separation and discrimination have all intensified difficulties between ethnic groups. Sometimes there is an ebb in the conflict, but a police beating or a discussion about affirmative action is all it takes for things to heat up again.

A friend of mine was ice skating in a public rink. A young boy bumped into him and others as he was being chased playfully. My friend said under his breath, "That black kid . . ." Then he caught himself and thought, *What does this kid's behavior have to do with him being black?*

Great question. The answer in this instance was—nothing. The kid was just being a kid. We are conditioned by our environment and experiences to prejudge or classify people in many ways. Some actions are influenced by our ethnicity, while others have nothing to do with it. We live in an era when there is heightened sensitivity to ethnic concerns and debate about what is the *right* way for different groups to relate. Movies like *Higher Learning*, *The Joy Luck Club* or *Mi Familia* all have something to say about relating with various ethnic groups. However, many ideas coming from the media, the academy and popular culture have no more bearing on Christian faith than does atheism. We must be solidly rooted in the biblical Christ and his message so we aren't swayed by false interpretations of Scripture. (Remember: American slavery was once justified from the Bible.)

To Get Started

The entire weight of Scripture falls on crushing the division, bitterness, hatred, injustice and indifference that exists between groups of people. Jesus' life, ministry and teaching, as well as the practice of the early church, support a direct and intentional assault on these things. They support unity, cooperative leadership, joint fellowship and compassionate concern for the needs of all groups. The gospel is the power of God to break hatred and divisions in the world. And the Spirit of God is the counselor who will guide us into this kind of life. The Scripture has but one position on this issue.

In Jesus' day and in Paul's, there were many ethnic groups that were hostile toward one another. Some of the most rigid and deepest divisions were between Jews and Gentiles and between Jews and Samaritans. These were rivalries that had long histories. Jewish rabbis would give thanks that they had not been born a Gentile or a dog. Jews would not eat food with Gentiles, much less sit at the same table with them or drink out of the same glass. They would not be welcome in each other's homes. Bands of Samaritans slaughtered Jewish travelers.

Jesus stepped into this world of overt hatred (much like the Middle East today or the United States during the Civil War). He made racial reconciliation central to becoming his disciple. *Racial reconciliation is the healing of these divisions by the power of God*. It is not a sidebar issue. It is central to the message of the gospel and at the heart of what it means to be a disciple.

In the New Testament
In only two places is Jesus directly asked "What must one do to inherit eternal life?" In Luke 10:25-37 he intentionally plays the race card in his answer. The *Cotton Patch Version,* a paraphrase of the Bible written in the context of the segregated South, captures the way this interaction and story would have been heard in Jesus' day.

One day a teacher of an adult Bible class got up and tested him with this question: "Doctor, what does one have to do to be saved?"

Jesus replied, "What does the Bible say? How do you interpret it?"

The teacher answered, "Love the Lord your God with all your heart and with all your soul and with all your physical strength and with all your mind; and love your neighbor as yourself."

"That is correct," answered Jesus. "Make a habit of this and you'll be saved."

But the Sunday school teacher, trying to save face, asked, "But . . . er . . . but just who *is* my neighbor?"

Then Jesus laid into him and said, "A man was going from Atlanta to Albany and some gangsters held him up. When they had robbed him of his wallet and his brand new suit, they beat him up and drove off in his car, leaving him unconscious on the shoulder of the highway.

"Now it just so happened that a white preacher was going down that same highway. When he saw the fellow, he stepped on the gas and went scooting on by.

"Shortly afterward a white, Gospel song leader came down the road, and when he saw what had happened, he too stepped on the gas.

"Then a black man traveling that way came upon the fellow, and what he saw moved him to tears. He stopped and bound up his wounds as best he could, drew some water from his water-jug to wipe away the blood and then laid him on the back seat. He drove on into Albany and took him to the hospital and said to the nurse, 'You all take good care of this white man I found on the highway. Here's the only two dollars I got, but you all keep account of what he owes, and if he can't pay it, I'll settle up with you when I make pay-day.'

"Now if you had been the man held up by the gangsters, which of these three—the white preacher, the white song leader, or the black man—would you consider to have been your neighbor?"

The teacher of the adult Bible class said, "Why of course, the nig . . . I mean, er . . . well, er . . . the one who treated me kindly."

Jesus said, "Well, then, *you* get going and start living like that."

All this amounts to: "You must be the kind of person who would radically love your ethnic enemies if you are to be saved." Can there be any stronger statement or motivation?

Jesus' general teaching about a life of faith also has meaning for cross-ethnic relations. His teaching on forgiveness in Matthew 18:15-35 has radical implications for those who have been wronged by racism. Yes you must forgive people—specifically the one(s) who wronged you. Better said, you must forgive if you expect to receive God's forgiveness. Furthermore, Jesus explicitly states that it is the love for enemies that distinguishes a disciple from others (Luke 6:27-36). A disciple both respects and recognizes the humanity of others regardless of how broken and twisted it may be. In 1 John 2:9 we read, "Whoever says, 'I am in the light,' while hating a brother or sister, is still in the darkness." If you do not love Christians of other ethnic groups, you are still in darkness and have not received the light of Christ. Ephesians 2:11-16 also tells us that as the first shining example of the new humanity offered to us, Jesus destroys the dividing wall of hostility between the Jews and Gentiles—the division that most concerned Paul and other apostles.

Time and time again, Jesus violated the ethnic taboos of his day by loving people who the Jews felt were losers. He made friends with those that his people hated. The Samaritan woman of John 4, the Syrophoenician woman of Mark 7 and the demoniac of Mark 5 are good examples.

Throughout his ministry Paul worked to eliminate the barriers between different ethnic groups in the church through his own example and through his teaching. As he shared the gospel throughout the New Testament world, Paul repeatedly urged Christians to uphold the integrity of the gospel message by loving hostile ethnic peoples. Paul even rebuked Peter for his hypo-

critical attitude in refusing to eat with the Gentile Christians when some
Jewish Christians showed up (Galatians 2). Evidently Peter was okay when
he was alone with the Gentiles, but when some of his own folks showed up,
he got a little uneasy and moved over to associate with them. After all, he
didn't want the fellas to think he was an Oreo. Paul saw this and made it
clear that this is not acceptable behavior, and it contradicts the very gospel
itself. A disciple of Christ must not be so easily swayed by the cares of the
world or those of their own ethnic group. In this Paul proved himself to be
a good friend to Peter.

In Acts the church at Antioch (Paul's home base for his missionary
efforts) was a great model for this message. It consisted of Jews and Gentiles, both in leadership and in general participation in the church (Acts
13:1).

Scripture is literally filled with passages that deal either implicitly or explicitly
with culture and ethnicity. Take an opportunity to look at these few:

Galatians 3:26-29. Since people cannot literally stop being Jewish and Gentile, what does it mean for Christians to disregard ethnicity? For example,
what might it mean to be Korean or Japanese or Mexican and yet disregard
ethnicity in terms of Christian fellowship?

Psalm 133. Have you ever felt the kind of joy that the psalmist is expressing
at witnessing this great unity?

John 17:20-23. What result comes from believers being unified across the
divisions of the world? When have you witnessed this?

Revelation 7:9-10. Who is present at this worship service? What does this
tell you about the goal of the work of God in the world? How can you align
yourself with this reality now as a disciple?

Only in Christ

Racial or ethnic issues were as much a part of the times of Jesus and Paul
as they are a part of our day. And we have *no excuse* for our resistance to,
lack of concern for and justification of the divisions in our world and in the
church today.

Racial reconciliation is only possible through the gospel. We must be
"in Christ" to receive the vision and strength to walk in this way. The Holy

Spirit enables believers to forgive and love people in ways different from the world. The great commission to take the gospel to *all* ethnic groups leaves no room for prejudicial evangelism or discipleship.

Racial reconciliation means exhibiting practical, costly love to people of a different ethnic group. It means being committed to the well-being and needs of others even more than our own needs (Philippians 2:3). It is about establishing deep relationships and fellowship, and commitments that are sincere and lasting. And it is about receiving the joy, blessing and power of God in our lives that cannot be experienced when the dividing walls still stand (Ephesians 2:14).

A disciple of Christ is one who even through struggle, awkwardness and unfamiliarity is willing to give everything in order to grow in this arena. What Jesus taught and lived is difficult. Paraphrasing G. K. Chesterton, Jesus' life and message have not been tried and found lacking. Rather, they have been found difficult and left untried.

One evening I went out to see the movie *Higher Learning* with some friends. Having bought the tickets in advance, two of us—a white woman and a black man—waited outside the theater until everyone made it in. The theater was packed, and so the two of us found seats toward the back of the theater. As the movie began, and as the unsettling scenes and issues rolled on, I realized that the majority of the audience was African American. Our group was mixed, including some Caucasians and Asian Americans—the only ones in the theater. At the end of the movie a black woman is shot and killed by a white racist, and a black man is unjustly beaten by white policemen. The black people in the theater exploded with rage at the scenes.

The movie ended and the lights came on. I was angry about what I had seen, and as people filed out past me, I grew uncomfortable sitting with a white woman in the middle of an all-black audience. She didn't understand how I felt, and I didn't want to explain it. I wanted to go find the black friends who were part of our group and hang with them. I didn't want to publicly associate with the white believers in our group. I was tempted to sin by rejecting my brothers and sisters in Christ because of what others might think or do. But I stayed—as I knew Jesus would. Later I talked through the experience with some of them.

I have not been welcomed in certain people's homes. I have endured the pains of injustice, been cursed at and had racial slurs hurled at me. I have been misunderstood by those who are well-intentioned but not part of my ethnic group. I have had to deal with anger, pain, frustration and hurt from such things. Various news reports and the foolish taunts of some public figures don't help. But I have found a deep reservoir of life in Jesus as I have taken steps to grow in this area.

I have had the honor of sharing life with believers from a variety of backgrounds. We have had to fight to understand each other at times. We have had to be patient and listen well, taking each other seriously. My aggressive confrontational style does not work well in public with my Korean American and Japanese American sisters. Loving them means being willing to speak in ways that enable them to better understand me. It also means they must work to adjust their ethnic ears to better understand me.

These are rich friendships that have exchanged a wealth of love for years now. We endured hard-fought battles with each other to become good and trusted friends, but the effort was worth it and true to the gospel. God has used each person and situation to enrich my life, helping me understand who he is and the richness of his kingdom.

Some Initial Steps

Develop a relationship with a believer who is very different from you. Learn about the history of his or her people. Try to see the world through his or her eyes.

Identify structural or institutional injustice against a particular ethnic group. How can you faithfully stand for justice?

Pray, asking God to reveal your hidden prejudices and whether there are groups you need to forgive.

If these are things you have done already, you will want to consider longer strides of faithfulness in deepening these relationships over time. Ask the Lord to guide you deeper into faithfulness in this area.

Living Your Faith

1. Growing up, what ethnic groups were you taught—subtly or overtly— were not as good as your own? What "messages" from your upbringing

need to be brought to Jesus for his approval or disapproval?

2. What ethnic groups are you least comfortable with?

3. How will you pray and cooperate with God to take steps that would bring reconciliation with someone in these ethnic groups?

Recommended Reading

More than Equals by Spencer Perkins and Chris Rice, InterVarsity Press.

Breaking Down Walls by Raleigh Washington and Glen Kehrein, Moody Press.

Strangers from a Different Shore: A History of Asian Americans by Ronald Takaki, Penguin.

eleven

Very Good Together
Amy Brooke

BRIAN STRUGGLED WITH CHOOSING HIS MAJOR. EVERYONE ASSUMED he would be premed. But when he compared the roles of doctors and nurses, he was drawn to the nursing side of medicine. Sure, he knew there were some male nurses, but nursing is a traditionally female role. What might his choice reflect about his masculinity? What will his friends say?

When Joan bought a car, she took Bill with her. Car salesmen always seem to respond better when a guy is there. She hated the stereotype of women not knowing anything about mechanics. She thought she might know a bit more than Bill. She appreciated Bill but resented the need to have him along.

The clothes in the baby section of the store were cute, but why did *everything* for a girl have to be so . . . *pink!* My sister had instructed me not to buy her daughter another pink outfit, but it was proving difficult. Two hours later I settled on a denim one-piece with white lace at the collar and two pink bows (which my sister could cut off) that was replete with pink and white hearts.

Gender Matters

From birth, gender matters. The first thing the doctor tells new parents (and the first thing new parents will be asked) is the gender of the child. Knowing the gender of the child is so important that those who make infant clothes have a system or code to provide clues. If the clothes are in neutral yellows and greens, then a pattern of footballs or flowers gives us a good hint. I'm grateful for any guidance when I'm unsure. Parents are insulted when their infant daughter is referred to as "a great big boy" or their son is called "a sweet princess." But it doesn't make picking out nonpink clothes easy.

Boys and girls start out much the same: eating and sleeping, but they grow up in "different" worlds. While there are more and more exceptions, generally boys are given toy trucks and sports equipment, and girls are given play tea sets and dolls. But children are not only given different things, the way they often play is different. In *You Just Don't Understand* researcher Deborah Tannen writes:

> Boys tend to play outside, in large groups that are hierarchically structured. Their groups have a leader who tells others what to do and how to do it, and resists doing what other boys propose. It is by giving orders and making them stick that high status is negotiated. . . . Boys' games have winners and losers and elaborate systems of rules that are the subject of arguments.
>
> Girls on the other hand, play in small groups or in pairs; the center of a girl's social life is a best friend. Within the group, intimacy is key: differentiation is measured by relative closeness. In their most frequent games, such as jump rope and hopscotch, everyone gets a turn. Many of their activities (such as playing house) do not have winners or losers.

So why do men and women act so differently? Are we different? Is that what God intended? Different cultures often prefer one gender over the other for various reasons. Does God like one gender more than the other?

A few years ago I would have balked at those questions. "We aren't all that different! God intended both sexes to just be human. People have created the differences." The truths I was missing were that our gender is a significant part of our humanity and gender is part of God's plan. As followers of Jesus we need to understand God's intention and the value of both halves of the human race.

God, Creation and Gender

God's plan for humanity is laid out in two accounts in Genesis. The first account (Genesis 1) gives us an overview. For five days God creates the heavens and the earth and all the plants and animals. After each day he looks around and says, "It is good."

On the sixth day God decides to create human beings. Genesis 1:27 says, "So God created humankind in his image, in the image of God he created them; male and female he created them." After this day of creation God looks at what he has done and sees that it is *"very good."* Men and women are equally created in God's image. Together they represent humankind. Humankind—men and women together—is God's crowning creation.

The more detailed account in Genesis 2 shows us an incompleteness in only having half of humankind. In this account the first man is surrounded only by the animals. And God declares that it is not good (the only "not good" in these first two chapters) for man to be alone. Thus God creates the first woman as a partner.

Is the woman an afterthought? From the first account we get no hint that she is. What is *very good* with her presence is *not good* without her. God does not make mistakes. He always planned to create the woman.

So why the second, detailed account? One reason is that whether male or female, our primary relationship is always with God. That is who the first man is primarily relating to at the beginning of creation. (Perhaps God knew of our propensity to make idols out of members of the opposite sex.) As Mary J. Evans writes in *Woman in the Bible,* the same is true of the first woman:

> Woman is created from the rib of the man, but it is important to note that it was the direct creative act of God in building up the rib that gave the woman her being, not the rib itself. She is "taken from the man," but, her first and primal contact is with her Maker. Woman herself knew God before she knew her counterpart, the man.

Second, the delay in the creation of the first woman means that there was a felt need. From the second account we see that men and women need each other. Without one gender there is an incompleteness in humanity as a whole. (Individual men and women are whole beings. It is humanity as a whole that is incomplete without both genders.) How much more must the man have valued the woman after initially being without her!

Their relationship is one of mutual trust and honesty. The author of Genesis tells us that at first they were both naked and unashamed. In other words, they were completely relaxed, open and unguarded around each other. Nothing marred that early relationship.

Into that paradise of complete freedom with each other—differences and all—came temptation. God had given them everything they needed. The only restriction was they were not to eat from the tree of the knowledge of good and evil. That one restriction was for their own protection. Whoever ate from it would die.

In Genesis 3 the serpent encourages the woman to go after the one thing that was forbidden. He plants a doubt about God's goodness, implying God is holding back the best from them. In spite of all they know about God, the pair eat from the tree. The result is that they realize their nakedness and try to hide away their differences from each other and God. No more easy freedom. There is shame in their relationship with each other and with God.

God informs the pair of three consequences. The collective consequence for humankind is banishment from the Garden of Eden, where everything was provided for them. The Garden of Eden also represented a place where they freely communed with each other and, more importantly, with God. From that point on there would always be a barrier between humankind and their Creator.

According to researcher Deborah Tannen, the important thing for men is often status or competence and for women it is relationship. Both men and women desire status and relationship to some degree, but this difference seems to be at the heart of the individual consequences in the Garden of Eden. The consequences of sin for the woman is increased pain in childbearing and a desire for her husband, who would rule over her. She desires an intimate relationship but instead gets a hierarchical relationship. For the man the consequence of sin is a relentless labor to master his uncooperative surroundings. The land that had willingly provided for his needs would now produce thorns and thistles. He is frustrated in his feelings of competence and status.

Like it or not, we reap the fruit of Adam and Eve's sin. It affects all of life and relationships. Throw into the "fruit bowl" our differences as men and women, and watch the lines in the sand be quickly drawn.

Boys will be boys. The differences discussed that first appear in childhood become significant in adulthood and cause misunderstandings. For example, there was a time when I was the only woman on a work team with several men. They were all great guys, and I usually really enjoyed being around them—one at a time. When with them in a group, however, I was often frustrated. They simply didn't "play" by the same rules that I did. They liked to decide things quickly. I wanted time to think and talk through all the possible aspects of the decision. I wanted to hear what everyone had to say, but they tended to talk over each other. Sometimes I hardly said anything because I was waiting for a turn to talk. While I eventually learned to jump in more, I often phrased my opinions more tentatively. As a result they often did not know how strongly I felt about something until I was angry.

Breaks from meetings exacerbated the situation. While I would have liked to go for a walk and chat, they consistently gravitated to the basketball hoop. Had I been sports-minded, it might have been different, but I ended up feeling isolated. Even when I tried to participate, I obviously brought the level of the game down. It was no one's fault. It was simply a different way of relating.

Men and women live in different "cultures." Whenever you are interacting with a different culture, there is the possibility of frustration, misunderstanding and hurt. The same principles that can help us in dealing with a different culture may be able to help us when dealing with those of the opposite gender.

Admonishment to Men
by Jonathan Tran

Let's face it, when it comes to how men have treated women, we won't be winning any trophies for Christlikeness. As a whole we have objectified, delegitimized, ostracized and raped the other half of God's image, forcing them into submission or separation. Sometimes we even use Scripture like Ephesians 5:24 ("Just as the church is subject to Christ, so also wives ought to be, in everything to their husbands") to justify our actions. The last time I looked,

Jesus never objectified, harassed, discriminated against, abused or neglected the church. We need to get our heads out of the sand, apologize, change our ways and learn with and from our kingdom partners. It is a matter of repentance.

InterVarsity's Student Training in Missions program (STIM) explains that the attitude with which we enter a crosscultural situation significantly influences the outcome. The same is true between genders. If we enter situations with suspicion, fear or prejudice, we experience frustration, anger and misunderstanding. To cope with these uncomfortable feelings we may become critical, rationalize our thoughts and actions, and isolate ourselves. The result is broken relationships. For example, several years ago I was significantly hurt in a battle over the role of women in ministry. A couple years later the topic came up with several people. I was suspicious of what one man was saying. We didn't agree, and I *read into* his statements unintended hostility and put-downs. I withdrew from the group. I needed to own up to the baggage I brought into the situation.

I've also had several conversations about the issue with men I trust. We don't always agree on every point. There have been misunderstandings because of what is said or the way it is said. However, in those situations, I listen and ask more questions. *I assume that even if we don't agree, this person is for me.* Our conversations led to a better understanding of each other and a strengthening of our relationship.

The difference in the situations lies in the attitude with which I entered the conversations. When we enter situations with a sense of trust and openness, there may be some frustration, irritation and misunderstanding. However, our initial attitudes help us cope through inquiry and listening. The relationship is then deepened through understanding and empathy.

If we accept the premise that conversations between men and women are crosscultural, it can help us give our counterparts grace. Instead of assuming something is a put-down, we might ask, How might another woman (or man) interpret that action or comment? We hesitate to think the worst and wonder instead if the opposite sex doesn't understand how their words and actions affect us. And we keep talking to clarify the issue.

STIM boils it down to a prior question of trust: Is what I am feeling, thinking or doing promoting trust? If the answer to any of those is no, what do I need to do to build trust? It's as simple as asking for clarification so you can understand where someone is coming from. It means occasionally participating in an activity that you don't like because the other person enjoys it. It means not telling "dumb blond" jokes or talking about how insensitive men are or not forwarding e-mail that stereotypes the other gender. Those things may seem innocent and funny (our culture does it readily), but they box in and criticize half of the population. They also offend God because they insult the dignity of his creation.

Primarily, the question of trust is about valuing the other person. It is determining to step into relationship with your best foot forward. It is having another's best interest at heart.

In *Children's Letters to God* a little girl writes, "Dear God, Do you like boys better than girls?" No, God doesn't like boys better than girls or girls better than boys. God knows that only together, as a reconciled whole, they are *very good.*

Living Your Faith

1. Do you think gender is important? Why or why not?

2. What evidence is there in Scripture that gender is important?

3. What evidence from your life supports the idea that male-female relationships are crosscultural?

4. How might the "prior question of trust" help you in your relationships?

5. When have you felt affirmed in your maleness or femaleness? How can you affirm another?

Recommended Reading

Equal to the Task by Ruth Haley Barton, InterVarsity Press.
Gender & Grace by Mary Stuart Van Leeuwen, InterVarsity Press.
You Just Don't Understand by Deborah Tannen, Ballantine.

twelve

Gone Too Far
Jonathan Tran

LOOK, LET'S BE HONEST. LET'S BE HONEST BECAUSE WHEN WE ARE, we live in light. When we're not, we live in darkness and learn to love evil.

So let's be real: *sexual sin wrecks faith lives.*

Compared to other sins, sexual sin reaps no greater condemnation from God. However, it leaves a wake of unparalleled destruction. Pornography, adultery, lust, romantic idolatry, homosexuality, various addictions and fornication are destroying our corporate spiritual body, one limb at a time.

How many times have we found ourselves captivated by pornographic images? How many times have we crossed *that* line with our boyfriend or girlfriend? How many times have we made the man or woman walking down the street an object of our lust?

We get tired of this: fighting these temptations and committing these sins. We get tired of saying to God, "Just this once more Lord, would you forgive me? I won't do it again." We get tired of having to read Psalm 51. We are tired of the shame, the frustration, the repeated confessions. We are tired of losing this battle, of having our otherwise sane faith lives wrecked. We are tired of feeling tired.

When I think of the Christian college students and young adults I have ministered to over the years, I am appalled at the frequency, scope and intensity of sexual and romantic sin. When I think about my own life, the addictions, the adulteries of the heart, the distortion of God-given wonder of sex, I am perplexed. As Paul said,

> I do not understand my own actions. For I do not do what I want, but I do the very thing I hate. Now if I do what I do not want, I agree that the law is good. But in fact it is no longer I that do it, but sin that dwells within me. For I know that nohting good dwells within me, that is, in my [sinful nature]. I can will what is right, but I cannot do it. For I do not do the good I want, but the evil I do not want is what I do. (Romans 7:15-19).

Sexual sin not only wrecks our individual faith lives, it also damages Christian community. It pushes us into dark corners where we cower in our own quiet desperation. Because we feel shamed and hopeless, we do not talk about our "private" struggle. We fight this battle alone, and consequently we lose it alone. Removed from the encouragement of our friends and the accountability of our community, we fight and lose. So we commit the sin and live in its destructive wake. The double casualty of sexual sin is the wrongful act and then the isolation it creates.

But there is hope. There is reason to continue fighting. This battle will not always result in defeat, shame and weariness. Jesus calls us to romantic and sexual holiness. It is a difficult call. Indeed, this call pushes us to the edge of our faith. Yet Jesus calls us, anticipating both defeats and ultimate victory.

The Cross

Jesus' call begins with the cross and the resurrection, where our depraved sexual sin meets God's amazing grace. Here the power of God smashes our hopelessness and powerlessness. Here our self-condemnation is overcome by Christ's cry, "It is finished" (John 19:30).

The cross is the only place where I can be real and honest. It is where I can stand before the congregation and say, "Yes, I have a bunch of dirty sins." It is where the congregation can respond, "That's right, and he died for those sins." It is the only place where I can confess that without shame and fear.

Yet the cross serves a notice—"Yes, Jon, your sin is that bad." The cross is the place where we realize that the consequence for our sexual sins is worse than we thought.

Michael and Joanna dated for six years. Like many Christian couples desiring holiness, they drew important physical affection boundaries. But each time a boundary was breached, they created boundaries that tolerated more sin. They reasoned, "We are having oral sex, but that is not *really* sex."

> *"Crucify him!" they shouted.*
> *"Why? What crime has he committed?" asked Pilate.*
> *But they shouted all the louder, "Crucify him!"*
> *Wanting to satisfy the crowd, Pilate released Barabbas [a terrorist convicted of murder] to them. He had Jesus flogged, and handed him over to be crucified.* (Mark 15:13-15 NIV)

Justin scrolled through the listed web sites. "Where's that one with those naked women?"

> *They stripped him and put a scarlet robe on him, and then twisted together a crown of thorns and set it on his head. They put a staff in his right hand and knelt in front of him and mocked him. "Hail, king of the Jews!" they said.* (Matthew 27:28-29 NIV)

Kato felt lonely after college. It was not like his tight-knit college fellowship that had helped him in his struggle with homosexuality. Here in the "real world" he had few true friends. There definitely was no accountability. So when he met Brian, the homosexual desires came back. He welcomed this new homosexual relationship which felt natural and good.

> *Carrying his own cross, he went out to the place of the Skull (which in Aramaic is called Golgotha). Here they crucified him, and with him two others one on each side and Jesus in the middle.* (John 19:17-18 NIV)

When Maria worked out at the gym, she could not help but look at all the guys. Some of them had the most incredible bodies, she thought. It did not help that most of them wore revealing clothes. She found herself coming to the gym just to check out men.

When the soldiers crucified Jesus, they took his clothes, dividing them into four shares, one for each of them, with the undergarment remaining. This garment was seamless, woven in one piece from top to bottom.
"Let's not tear it," they said to one another. "Let's decide by lot who will get it."
This happened that the scripture might be fulfilled which said,
"They divided my garments among them
and cast lots for my clothing."
So this is what the soldiers did. (John 19:23-24 NIV)

Though Greg had not seen a porn movie since he became a Christian, the images of sex stayed with him. These images always led to fantasizing and then to masturbation. He felt most vulnerable while taking a shower. He told himself to not think about those things. He even started playing Christian CDs during showers. For a time he stopped taking showers all together. No matter what he tried, nothing seemed to work. Greg was addicted to masturbation.

In the same way the chief priests, the teachers of the law and the elders mocked him. "He saved others," they said, "but he can't save himself! He's the King of Israel! Let him come down now from the cross." (Matthew 27:41-42 NIV)

Janet loved Nathan. Never had she felt so loved before. Never had any person, any man, given her so much attention. He made her feel so valuable and beautiful. They began each day with breakfast together and said good-bye only late into the night. They attended the young adult fellowship together and even did their quiet times with each other. People always talked about how they made the perfect couple. What they didn't see was how Nathan had replaced God in her life.

And at the ninth hour Jesus cried out in a loud voice, "Eloi, Eloi, lama sabachthani?"—*which means, "My God, my God, why have you forsaken me?* (Mark 15:34 NIV)

George and Debbie were having an affair. Debbie had been married to Tim only two years. Yet already she found herself so much happier with George. She knew she could never divorce Tim, for she was a Christian, and she could not handle the humiliation of confessing. She wanted to protect Tim, but she wanted to be with George.

Darkness came over the whole land until the ninth hour, for the sun stopped shining. And the curtain of the temple was torn in two. Jesus called out with a loud voice, "Father, into your hands I commit my spirit." When he had said this, he breathed his last. (Luke 23:44-46 NIV)

The Resurrection
The resurrection says to us, Yes it was that bad, but now it is better, much better. Though we died because of sin, sin no longer has the power of death over us. Jesus handles our indecent indulgences with his death and resurrection.

Repentance—not the shamed, self-absorbed, feeling-bad-about-myself-to-no-avail variety but the get-off-your-rear-and-pull-a-U-turn kind—is possible for us, offered to us and demanded of us. Only the resurrection gives us this hope. It tells us that we can and should do something.

Michael and Joanna drew a new line. No more touching, other than holding hands. They realized that asking the question How far can we go in satisfying our physical desires? was the wrong question. Instead, they began to ask, How much do I want to present this person blameless and holy to God? How much do I want to control myself to serve this person? How much do I want to follow Jesus in my dating relationship?

Very early on the first day of the week, just after sunrise, they were on their way to the tomb and they asked each other, "Who will roll the stone away from the entrance of the tomb?"

But when they looked up, they saw that the stone, which was very large, had been rolled away. (Mark 16:2-4 NIV)

After receiving much prayer and guidance from his faith community, Justin confessed to his bosses at work that he had been looking at pornographic sites on the Internet during working hours. He committed to making up lost hours. He asked their forgiveness, and he asked them to monitor his Internet use.

As they entered the tomb, they saw a young man dressed in a white robe sitting on the right side, and they were alarmed.

"Don't be alarmed," he said. "You are looking for Jesus the Nazarene, who was crucified. He has risen!" (Mark 16:5-6 NIV)

Kato called Evan, an accountability partner from his college days. It took a long time to get it out, but he confessed his homosexual relationship. Evan cried as Kato related his loneliness and predicament. He also told him that God had forgiven him and was proud of him for confessing. They discussed options for Christian community. Immediately, Kato ended his homosexual relationship.

"Why do you look for the living among the dead? He is not here; he has risen! Remember how he told you, while he was still with you in Galilee: 'The Son of Man must be delivered into the hands of sinful men, be crucified and on the third day be raised again.'" (Luke 24:5-7 NIV)

Maria stopped going to the gym. She bought some exercise videos and worked out at home. She also worked on looking people in the eyes and getting to know them as people, not just bodies. She joined a small group at her church that talked openly about sexual sin.

Then Simon Peter, who was behind him, arrived and went into the tomb. He saw the strips of linen lying there, as well as the burial cloth that had been around Jesus' head. The cloth was folded up by itself, separate from the linen. Finally the other disciple, who had reached the tomb first, also went inside. He saw and believed. (John 20:6-8 NIV)

Greg told his young adult Bible study group about his past experiences with pornography. They prayed that God would take those images away.

Amazingly, those images came around less often. Whenever Greg fell into masturbation, he confessed to his roommates. In addition, they held Greg accountable by frequently asking him how he was doing with his showers.

So they went out quickly from the tomb with fear and great joy, and ran to bring his disciples word.
And as they went to tell his disciples, behold, Jesus met them, saying, "Rejoice!" (Matthew 28:8-9 NKJV)

After a church sermon on idolatry Janet felt convicted that she should break up with Nathan. Though it was the hardest thing she had ever done, it was amazingly good. She learned to fall in love with Jesus, to be wooed and loved by him. She found that Jesus was a tremendous friend and life partner as well as Lord and Savior. The loss of Nathan took several years to get over, but at the same time she grew to love Jesus more than any person.

They came to him, clasped his feet and worshiped him. Then Jesus said to them, "Do not be afraid. Go and tell my brothers to go to Galilee; there they will see me." (Matthew 28:9-10 NIV)

After reading about David and Bathsheba (2 Samuel 11), Debbie ended her relationship with George. Next she painfully confessed the whole affair to Tim.

Tim cried and hurt terribly. He told her that he forgave her and asked her to commit anew to him. Each night Tim would crawl out of bed and pray at Debbie's feet that God would grow in her a new love for their relationship. Debbie began meeting with a Christian counselor who helped explore generational sins of adultery in her family's history. God blessed their hard work, and they grew more in love than ever.

Then he opened their minds so they could understand the Scriptures. He told them, "This is what is written: The Christ will suffer and rise from the dead on the third day, and repentance and forgiveness of sins will be preached in his name to all nations." (Luke 24:45-47 NIV)

Beware the Spider's Web!

Pornography is easily accessible on the Web. Simply ask your search engine to find pornography and it will. Even if you aren't looking for it, you may accidentally stumble on a "cyberporn" site. Once you've found it, it's easy to find it again. And again. If you have a free, fast, private Internet connection, as do most college dorm rooms and business offices, then you have quick, private access to a world of pornography. Soon you may find yourself stuck in this spider's web. Here are a few suggestions.

☐ Invest in an Internet security program. "Net Nanny," "Cyberpatrol" and "Kid's Desk Internet" are all recommended. The problem with most of these programs is they are made for children, so they are easy to bypass. Have your friend install it. That way you will not know the bypass password, and you will not be familiar with the bypass procedures.

☐ Some Internet providers are either religion- or education-affiliated. These providers provide Web services with built-in safeguards. Contact local elementary schools or Christian radio stations and bookstores to find such providers.

☐ Consider not having a connection to the Web. Hook up with Juno.com or other free e-mail providers. You can still surf the Web from a friend's computer, from the school or from the local library. Who needs all that information anyway?

☐ Have a friend regularly check your computer to see which Web sites you have been visiting. Most computers and Internet programs provide a list of the last dozen or more Web sites visited. The fear of your friend seeing where you've been will keep you honest.

Living Your Faith

1. Of the several scenarios in this chapter, which of them do you relate to the most? In what ways is your "scenario" similar and in what ways is it different?

2. Which of the biblical passages about Jesus' crucifixion speaks to the price he paid for your particular sin?

3. In the resurrection section we read of how these fellow believers sought help and solutions for their dilemmas. Can one or more of them work for you?

4. How does the resurrection of Jesus give us hope of victory with our sexual sins?

5. What friend might you discuss your struggles with? When can that happen?

Recommended Reading

I Loved a Boy/I Loved a Girl by Walter Trobisch, InterVarsity Press.

Eros Defiled by John White, InterVarsity Press.

Eros Redeemed by John White, InterVarsity Press.

God, Sex & the Search for Lost Wonder by Mike Starkey, InterVarsity Press.

True Love in a World of False Hope by Robbie Castleman, InterVarsity Press

thirteen

Loving Your Parents
Paul Tokunaga

THINK ABOUT MICHELANGELO PAINTING THE CEILING OF THE SIStine Chapel. *Over four years flat on his back, contorting his body and painstakingly guiding his brushes to paint in a manner he was unaccustomed to.*

Loving your parents is something like that. It's unlike the way you love anyone else in the world. It has to be done differently. It's a very sophisticated art form. It's a very sophisticated, s-l-o-w art form. It's a very sophisticated, slow, *learned* art form. It doesn't just happen. It takes patience, discipline and a long time to do it well.

Here's the Rub

As disciples of Jesus we are to love our parents. For some of us it's not a problem—always have, always will. They love us; we love them. We'd spend every vacation, every weekend with them if we could. On to the next chapter, please. For others, it's hard to imagine loving them. Forget vacations. We don't even want to be in the same room with them.

Perhaps something happened back in your childhood (or not so far back) that is like a pebble in your shoe. You were injured, abused, misunderstood, betrayed, manipulated or abandoned. You told yourself, *The hurt and anger will eventually go away. I just need to give it time.* But like the pebble, it has stayed with you. You feel it with every step. Leave it there and eventually it will poke a hole through your protective sock and start cutting into your flesh. Mom (or Dad, or both) has hurt you, and you can't forgive and forget. Or you've tried to forgive with your heart, but your mind can't forget.

Still others are somewhere in between: not quite the Cosby family but not quite *Married with Children* either. We love our parents, but it lacks passion. To be truthful, it feels a little dutiful: I'm supposed to love my parents, so I will.

How can we love our parents more? Here are five things that might be helpful.

One: Believe That God Gave You Your Family

Pull out that family portrait and give it a good stare. Do you ever feel God made a mistake by putting you in your family? Do you sometimes feel that you just don't fit?

Has your family ever embarrassed you? Here are four of my most "embarrassing things about my family" as I grew up:

☐ *All my friends are white.* How did I come out Japanese?

☐ *All my friends seem to be Catholic or Methodist.* Why did I have to be born into a Buddhist family? How do I ever explain the mysterious chants in Japanese and all that incense burning?

☐ *My parents don't go to PTA meetings or my baseball games.* Don't they care about the most important parts of my life?

☐ The ultimate hardship for me was *I wanted to be in Gary Tomasso's family.*

Gary was an only child. He always had great stuff, like a Peugeot 12-speed bike. I had a 10-speed Huffy. He always wore Levi's. My jeans came from J. C. Penney. His first car was a Malibu Super Sport with 396 cubic inches. Mine was a 36-horsepowered VW Karmann Ghia, which girls called "cute." I hated cute.

I never measured up to Gary.

Many years after becoming a Christian I began to realize: *God gave me my family.* He never intended me to be in Gary Tomasso's family. Verses like Psalm 139:16 helped: "In your book were written all the days that were formed for me, when none of them as yet existed."

What about you? Do you believe God loves you? Do you believe he gave you your family *because he loves you—even if they aren't followers of Jesus?* Until we can say *yes,* life will be like wearing very dark sunglasses. We will be unable to see clearly how God is at work in our lives and in our family's lives.

Two: Scripture Gives Some Guidelines

If we can say God has a purpose in putting us in the family we're in, has he left us without clear-cut instructions on how to treat our parents? Has he given us the ingredients but left us without the recipe? Answers: no and yes. First, the no.

Scripture is fairly silent on the specifics of how we should treat our parents. At times I yearn for some "direct directives":

☐ Thou shalt ask thy parents' permission with whom thou shalt go out with next Friday, and thou shalt be in by 11:30 p.m.

☐ When thou visit thy family home, thou shalt help Mother with dishes on Mondays, Wednesdays and Fridays, but not on Tuesdays and Thursdays.

☐ Thou shalt call home—and not dialing collect—every weekend.

Scripture offers few such specific directives. The clearest directive is one that runs throughout the Old and New Testaments: *honor your parents.* Scripture breaks that down for us by telling us we shouldn't attack or curse our fathers or do foolish things or rob our parents. We shouldn't despise our mothers, and daughters shouldn't rise up against mothers— things like that.

But here's the *yes.* He does give us instructions. *Scripture is hardly silent on how we treat people.* Sometimes, we have two categories: how I treat people, and how I treat my parents. We need to see that *everything in Scripture about how we treat people applies to how we treat our parents.*

Here are two mini-Bible studies to do sometime.

Take 2 Corinthians 1:3-7. This is Paul's comfort chapter. God is the ultimate comforter. Like him, we should comfort others. Paul uses the word *console* (or comfort) ten times in these five verses. *Console* best means "to walk alongside another person in their trouble." Bible expositor Earl Palmer says that "the word 'console' in this passage is most accurately described like this: a person is walking down a road alone, and he is then joined by another who walks alongside so he does not have to walk the rest of the way alone" (Rebecca Manley Pippert, *Out of the Saltshaker*).

How might this sound if we relate it to our parents? It would go something like this: "Blessed be the God who has walked alongside us, who walked alongside us in our affliction, so that we may be able to walk alongside Mom and Dad in their affliction with all the 'walking-alongsideness' that we have experienced." How can we now walk alongside Mom and Dad?

For a second study *take 1 Corinthians 13* and focus the qualities of love onto your relationship with Mom and Dad. Verses 4-7, for starters, would go like this for me:

"Paul is patient toward Mom;
Paul is kind toward Dad.
Paul is not envious or boastful or arrogant or rude toward Mom and Dad.
Paul doesn't insist on his own way with Mom.
Paul is not irritable or resentful toward Dad.
Paul bears all things with Mom;
Paul endures all things with Dad."

Then comes the hard part of any good Bible study—ask yourself, "What specific actions could I take for each of these things to come true in my relationship with Mom or Dad?" Ouch.

In your own personal Bible study and devotions, when you come to passages that tell you how to treat others, put the spotlight on Mom and Dad.

Three: Part of Love Is Showing Appreciation

What can we compare to being a parent? For twenty or thirty years (give or take a few), your parents have done all they could for you, and for the most part they probably don't even know what you really think of them.

Being a parent is like holding your breath for twenty years, waiting to hear what your kids think of you.

Here are nine things you can do to get them breathing again:

Thank them for something . . . anything.

Think about what God has done in you through them. You are profoundly like them, like it or not. Think of something good in your emotions, skills or intellect. Thank them.

"Anything I can do when I come home?" Ask in an e-mail or phone home before you arrive. Don't just be a freeloader when home.

Make a meal you've learned. It may not be as good as Mom's or Dad's, but it can serve as a bridge between home and your world now. If you really want to impress them, buy the ingredients yourself.

Block out some prime time. Share what you are learning at school or at work; tie it into things they taught you at home.

Learn your parents' stories: what their childhood was like and how they met. What big events shaped their lives? What were they like at your age?

Take your siblings out for a game, shopping or a movie. Let them know you still care. Talk "family talk" with them. Be sure to ask, "How do you think Mom and Dad are doing?"

Clean your room when you leave.

Kiss your mom and hug your dad when you arrive and leave.

Four: Learn Your Parents' Language of Love

My parents love me, but it took me well over twenty years to realize it. My first physical contact with Dad came when I left for college and he shook my hand. I considered not washing it. Our first hug came when I was about thirty. Mom and Dad never have told me they love me or are proud of me. But I know, without any doubt, they *do* love me and *are* proud of me.

They simply speak a different language of love. They show their love in different ways. In a recent poll taken by Tokunaga Touchy-Feely-Warm-Fuzzies Analysts, Inc., it was discovered that Asian American parents score second lowest on the touchy-feely scale, barely beating out residents of Fargo, N.D., in January.

If Asian American parents scored second, then fathers with daughters were a close third. It's awkward for a dad to know how to express affection to his "little girl" who is now a grown woman. Give him grace and a hug.

When I would visit home during college years, Dad would almost always slip $20 into my pocket as I left to go back to school. It used to really bug me. *He's trying to buy me off. Why can't he just hug me? That's worth more than $20 to me.* It never bugged me enough to refuse it, however.

Some parents often show their love through money. It's tangible to them. They worked hard to earn it. Whenever you doubt their love for you, say to yourself five times slowly, "$100,000" or "$20,000" or "$50,000"—whatever it costs them to send you through college. Multiply that number by the number of children in your family. They *chose* to give it to you. They didn't have to. Have you ever heard them grumble about what cruises they could have taken or dream house purchased if they didn't send you to college?

Figure out your Mom's and your Dad's love languages. Learn to receive their expressions of love graciously. (In his *Losing Face & Finding Grace* Bible study guide [InterVarsity Press], Tom Lin has a very helpful study on "Languages of Love: Communicating with Our Parents More Effectively.")

Five: Parents Do Make Mistakes and They Need to Be Forgiven
Parents sometimes blow it badly, do stupid things, can be awfully irrational and are not half as bright as their children. Now that we're clear on the facts, we can move on.

A good friend related this "Mom story":

"Mom is a great cook. Growing up, she liked to try new dishes on us. Most were successes. One was not: 'boiled squid *au jus'*—as in boiled in his own inky juice. I was in high school, much more enamored with pizza and double cheeseburgers. I tried, I really did, but I just could not eat it.

"Mom said I couldn't leave the table until I ate it. I stared at it. It stared at me. We were becoming friends. I couldn't eat my friend. I sat there until close to ten o'clock. Finally she gave up and let me go to bed.

"About twenty years later I was visiting home. Out of the blue, Mom sort of blurted out, 'I made you eat squid once. I shouldn't have done it.' I was stunned. *This had been bothering her for twenty years.* I wish I had known so I could have forgiven her when I was fifteen, not thirty-five."

Dad worked day and night selling life insurance. He came home at 5:00 p.m.; dinner was always on the table at 5:15. He'd snooze a bit after dinner in his favorite TV chair and be out the door by 7:00, calling on potential customers until about 10:00. He worked hard because he wanted his family to have more than what he had growing up. There were lots of mouths to feed, shirts to buy and college funds to which to contribute.

My first and only love growing up was baseball. I ate and breathed the game. Dad was working so much he didn't come to my games. My last year in Little League we had a very special game against the league-leading Campbell Stamps. We were chosen to play in Bees Stadium, the home of the Angels Class A farm team. Big stuff! I was so proud to have Dad finally see me play.

I played center field for the Knights of Pythias (don't ask me what a Pythias is). I got two hits off Bobby Rasmussen, one of the best pitchers in the league. The game ended. I felt good. I was ready for Dad to congratulate me on my hitting. Instead: "You missed that fly ball in center. You should have charged it. You could have caught it." I was devastated. He didn't say a word about my two hits. I never asked him to come to another game again. I couldn't risk the pain.

Dad made a mistake, and I held it against him for years. It got in the way of my loving him. Whenever I talked about that game with friends, I would choke up. It hurt even more when he went to almost all of my younger brother's games and would come home excited about his play.

When did I finally forgive him? When I started going to my son Sam's games. I vowed I would go to his games. That was easy. I still love baseball. I even helped coach his teams. The hard part came when we would drive home. It would take everything in me to not say, "You missed that fly ball." Or, "You took a called strike three." It was incredibly hard to stop myself and to find things he did right.

Even when Sam would ask, "How did you like my double?" I would bite my tongue to not say, "You could have stretched it into a triple if you had run harder." *That's when I really forgave Dad,* when I realized, as a father, how hard it was not to correct my son. What I couldn't see back then, I see now: Dad wanted me to be better. He saw the potential, but I just heard, "Bad play! You gave up!" Dad knew I could have caught that ball if I had charged it. But I couldn't see that. All I could see was that I was a failure in his eyes.

Loving our parents means we quit holding their humanness against them. We let them be fallible, like us. We give them room to grow. We give them grace. Loving them means we put away the list of things in our minds they've done wrong and not hold it against them. *One of the greatest weapons we have to use against our parents is withholding forgiveness.*

God wants your parents to experience forgiveness from any place they can get it, including from you—*especially* from you.

Listen to God

"Bear with one another and, if anyone has a complaint against another, forgive each other, just as the Lord has forgiven you, so you also must forgive" (Colossians 3:13). Even our parents.

"Be kind to one another, tenderhearted, forgiving one another, as God in Christ has forgiven you" (Ephesians 4:32). Even our parents.

Is your heart like a knotted-up fist, full of anger, bitterness or resentment toward your mom or dad? Pray this prayer:

Lord, I can't do it. I can't forgive them. I've been hurt too deeply. But, I put my heart in your grip. Lord, I give you the authority to loosen the knotted fist of my heart. But you have to do it. I can't.

That's a start. That's enough for God to go to work. If you do that, share it with a good friend who can pray with you and for you.

Nobody said loving your parents would be a piece of cake. It takes hard work and a lot of prayer. It takes forgiveness and offering grace.

God loves it when you love them. It honors the decision he made to put you in your family.

Thank you, God, for making me a Tokunaga and letting me be in this family.

Living Your Faith

1. Do you truly believe God put you in your family because he loves you?

2. Do the mini-Bible studies in 1 Corinthians 1:37 and 1 Corinthians 13.

3. When will you see your parents next? What specific things can you do to show your appreciation for them? (Use the list in "Three: Part of Love Is Showing Appreciation" for ideas.)

4. What is your parents' language of love for you?

5. Do you need to forgive your parents for anything?

Recommended Readings

Following Jesus Without Dishonoring Your Parents by Jeanette Yep et al., InterVarsity Press.

Forgiving Our Parents, Forgiving Ourselves by David Stoop and James Masteller, Servant.

Recovery from Family Dysfunctions (Life Recovery Guide), InterVarsity Press.

part three

Disturbing the World

"Change always disturbs."
JOHN F. KENNEDY

"The only thing necessary for the triumph of evil is for
the good [person] to do nothing."
EDMUND BURKE

"I am willing to fail. Risks are not to be evaluated
in terms of the probability of success but in terms
of the value of the goal."
RALPH WINTER

"Discipleship is built entirely on the supernatural grace of
God . . . to live 24 hours in every day as a saint,
to go through the drudgery as a disciple, to live
an ordinary, unobserved, ignored existence as a
disciple of Jesus. It is inbred in us that we have to
do the exceptional things for God, but we have not. We
have to be holy in the mean streets, among mean people,
and this is not learned in five minutes."
OSWALD CHAMBERS

"For the Son of Man came not to be served but to serve,
and to give his life as a ransom for many."
JESUS CHRIST

fourteen

Redeeming Every Square
Inch of Creation
Bobby Gross

G IVE UP YOUR SMALL AMBITIONS," URGED THE MISSIONARY LEADER speaking to our InterVarsity spring conference. "Why would you wrap yourself in the American flag and work at some job all your life just so you could retire in a comfortable house filled with beautiful things when you could be crossing cultures in order to build the kingdom of God?"

I was a university senior and this challenge fired me up. At the time I was weighing two options, either going to law school or joining InterVarsity staff as a prelude to missionary work in China.

The pull toward law school had more to do with the prospect of prestige, income and parental approval than with any real interest in the practice of law or the American justice system. In my first years of college God had already nailed me on three hidden idolatries in my life: materialism, racism and nationalism. I was ripe for the appeal to choose ministry over law. Twenty-two years later I still serve on the staff of InterVarsity—with no regrets. Looking back, however, I do think the conceptual framework in which I made my choice was somewhat skewed.

The speaker was right to confront our attraction to material goods and comfort, to question our knee-jerk patriotism and to hold out the importance of crosscultural missions. He was wrong, however, to suggest that ministry or missionary work is a higher calling than, say, law or business or politics. He seemed to represent a way of thinking that maintains a dichotomy between the "sacred" and the "secular." But God does not see it that way, as we will discover.

The Bible, taken as a whole, tells one grand story. It begins in Genesis with God creating the cosmos, including humanity made in his image, and ends in Revelation with God making a new heaven and earth. In between, of course, the story tells how things went so terribly wrong for humanity and the world, and unfolds God's plan to do something about it. It is a plan of *redemption,* that is, the "buying back" or restoration of what was lost or damaged. The plan centers on the great Redeemer, Jesus. All who follow Jesus become part of the story in anticipation of the glorious culmination when he returns.

This grand story provides the framework for exploring our main question in this chapter: what is the scope of God's redemptive purposes in the world and what is our part in these? Is the world like a burning house from which God primarily is intent on rescuing the trapped inhabitants? Or is God also intent on saving the house, that is, dousing the flames and rebuilding the structure so that people can once again make their home within it?

I am convinced of the latter. God not only loves and seeks to save all humanity; he also loves his fallen creation, including human culture, and seeks to redeem it as well. Consequently, we have a two-fold mandate as God's people: to embody and proclaim the gospel everywhere in the world so that men and women are reconciled to God, and to live as a transforming presence in the world so that all aspects of life increasingly come under the leadership of Christ. Thus God is just as interested in Christian lawyers as he is in Christian missionaries!

In the Beginning
"In the beginning, God created the heavens and the earth" (Genesis 1:1).

God brought the cosmos into being out of nothing. He spoke and there was light and sky and land and seas. God further developed what he had made by separating, bringing forth and naming. At each stage God looked at his creative work and with satisfaction pronounced it good. He liked what he saw!

The doctrine of creation is rich with significance and implications. Here are a few:

☐ God and the creation are no more synonymous than a painter and her painting are. Creation reflects God's glory (Psalm 19:1) but is not divine in itself and is not to be worshiped (Romans 1:25).

☐ There is nothing inherently evil about the material world. God delights in stars and trees and animals—he made them, after all.

☐ The Creator owns the world, we don't: "The earth is the Lord's and all that is in it" (Psalm 24:1).

☐ God is no absentee landlord. He actively rules the cosmos as Creator-King. In fact, "he sustains all things by his powerful word" (Hebrews 1:3).

"God created humankind in his image . . . male and female he created them" (Genesis 1:27). Human beings are the crown of creation. No other creature is made "in God's image." But what exactly does this mean? The answer likely includes multiple dimensions of our humanity such as rationality, morality and spirituality. Two other dimensions especially stand out: the capacity for loving relationships and the capacity for responsible stewardship. We image God when we love one another as he loves and when we act in the world as he acts.

We learn from Genesis that God blessed humanity and gave us a multifaceted mandate. We are to "be fruitful and multiply, and fill the earth" (1:28). We are to "subdue the earth and have dominion over it" (1:28). Speaking of the first garden, we were to "till it and keep it" (2:15). Finally, we were to name the creatures (2:18-20). In short, we have been blessed with the privilege of stewardship of creation. A steward is one who manages property or affairs on behalf of an owner. Marvelously, God has chosen to work out his plans for creation through humans. However, we are not free to act autonomously.

First, our stewardship of creation is a corporate one. God designed us to be in relationships. The only thing "not good" in creation was Adam's aloneness, so God made the woman to be his partner. From this initial cohumanity, we can extrapolate God's intentions that there be marriage, family, friendship, community and society. We are stewards together.

Second, to *subdue* the earth does not mean to exploit it but rather to bring order to it, to develop its potential. And to *rule* the earth does not mean to enslave or destructively control but to serve the interests of and care for it. The task of Adam and Eve in the garden helps clarify these roles. They were to *till,* or cultivate, the garden and they were to *keep,* or preserve, it. No room here for polluting or destroying the environment, rather the environment was to be a source of provision and an opportunity for stewardship.

God's intention from the beginning was for men and women together to image him by growing into a full human society and by developing the full potential of creation in human culture. *Cultivate* and *culture* are closely linked in meaning as Brian Walsh and Richard Middleton explain:

> Besides gardens, we also cultivate relationships, manners, and forms of worship. We harness animals and forces of nature. We formulate and develop ideas and traditions, and we construct not only technological objects but social groupings and institutions as well. All these activities and their results are cultural; that is they are humanly developed realities . . . . To be a cultural being is, quite simply, to be human. *(The Transforming Vision)*

We were created to live in loving relationship with our Creator and to bring glory to him by loving one another and fulfilling his purposes for creation. He envisioned science and art and government and family from the start. He started humans out in a garden, but he destined us to end in a great city! Something, however, went wrong.

A Fatal Choice

When the original humans, in response to temptation from the serpent, chose to disregard God's wisdom and ways and to assert their own autonomy, everything was affected: humans were alienated from their Creator, from one another and from their environment. No longer could they fulfill their "cultural mandate" with a joyful ease: childbirth would be painful, marriage would be unbalanced, work would be toilsome and life span would be limited. Nonetheless, the opportunity and responsibility to act as stewards of creation was not withdrawn. The image of God in humans has been distorted but not destroyed, and the goodness of creation has been tainted but not obliterated.

The world is now an ambiguous place for us. On one hand, it is still God's good creation, which he lovingly sustains. On the other, it is a dangerous place under the influence of Satan and laced with evil, injustice and temptation. Due to the Fall, human culture is corrupt and falls short of God's original design.

This is why in Scripture the term *world* carries two different meanings. One refers to the cosmos, that is, the creation that belongs to God. The other refers to humanity in its fallenness and resistance to God. Thus many passages speak of the world in negative terms (for example, John 14:30; Colossians 2:20; James 4:1-4). Jesus prayed for his followers, "I am not asking you to take them out of the world, but I ask you to protect them from the evil one. They do not belong to the world, just as I do not belong to the world" (John 17:15-16). It is important to distinguish between the world as God's creation and the world as humanity organized against God. We are to be *in* the cosmos but not *of* its fallen nature.

The Turning Point

God, full of grace, began his redemptive response to our sin right after the Fall of the original humans. He clothed Adam and Eve, and he promised that Eve's offspring would strike the serpent's head in the ensuing centuries. He unfolded his redemptive plan through the making of covenants with Abraham and the other patriarchs, the choosing and shaping of Israel as a nation, and the sending of prophets, priests and kings. In these ways God revealed more and more of himself and his will for humanity.

But ultimately redemption came through Jesus Christ. God's Son became human and entered our history. He proclaimed and enacted the kingdom of God, gave his life for us on the cross, rose in triumph over the powers of darkness, and now sits enthroned in heaven, destined to return and consummate his kingdom. "He has rescued us from the power of darkness and transferred us into the kingdom of his beloved Son, in whom we have redemption, the forgiveness of sins" (Colossians 1:13-14).

Jesus' purpose extends beyond the salvation of human beings, as Paul goes on to proclaim in Colossians 1:15-20:

> He is the image of the invisible God, the firstborn of all creation; for in him all things in heaven and on earth were created, things visible and invisible, whether thrones or dominions or rulers or powers—all things have been created through him and for him. He himself is before all things, and in him all things hold together. He is the head of the body, the church; he is the beginning, the firstborn from the dead, so that he might come to have first place in everything. For in him all the fullness of God was pleased to dwell, and through him God was pleased to reconcile to himself all things, whether on earth or in heaven, by making peace through the blood of his cross.

Jesus was involved in the creation of *all things*. Jesus entered his creation through the incarnation and thus affirms and completes it. Jesus, through his death, not only redeems humanity but also reconciles *all things* back to God.

A Transforming Presence

We who follow Jesus are ambassadors for the kingdom of God and agents of transformation in the world. First, we have an *evangelistic mandate*. We communicate the gospel, the message of reconciliation, among all the peoples of the earth, starting with our friends and neighbors. We proclaim it through who we are, how we live and what we say. Not all are evangelists or pastors or missionaries, but we all *must* be ambassadors and witnesses. Furthermore, the church is a witnessing community in which we seek to live out our lives together under the leadership of Jesus.

Second, we have a continuing *cultural mandate*. We are part of human society exercising a stewardship over God's creation in all its dimensions. God remains intensely interested in "all things." He is glorified when we act to develop the potential of the created order and when we care for creation in line with his purposes.

He wants us to be *light* that dispels what is evil in the world and *salt* that enhances and preserves what is good. He wants us to forsake all idolatries that usurp his place in our lives and oppose all powers that thwart his purposes in the world. He wants us to bring every aspect of our lives under his leadership. He wants us to be his transforming presence wherever we live and work.

Consider three from among the many areas for application. First, *environmental stewardship*. In light of the current ecological crises such as deforestation, habitat destruction, endangered species, ozone depletion and global warming, what voice and role do we, as Christians, need to exercise as those who know the Creator and love the creation?

Second, *academic studies*. If you are a student, your challenge is to "think Christianly" about your field of study. This calls for a thoughtful integration of Scripture and theology with your academic discipline. If you do not actively develop a Christian worldview, you will simply absorb those of your professors and peers. You will become conformed to the unredeemed thought patterns of this world rather than "renewing your mind" so as to be a transforming presence within academia (see Romans 12:2).

Third, *vocational choices*. In light of our fundamental vocation, or calling, to be bearers of the gospel and stewards of creation, we now understand that a wide range of work will bring honor to God and advance his redemptive plans in the world. God might guide you to become a missionary or a campus minister. Or he might lead you to be a sculptor or educator or homemaker or lawyer. For we understand, in the famous words of Abraham Kuyper, "There is not one square inch of the entire creation about which Jesus Christ does not cry out 'this is mine!'"

The End of the Story
"The kingdom of this world has become the kingdom of our Lord and of his Messiah and he will reign forever and ever," declares the chorus of voices in Revelation 11:15, foretelling the end of the grand story. Indeed, the final chapters of the Bible depict the new heaven, the new earth and the New Jerusalem. God will make his home among us, his people. He will

wipe every tear from our eyes. There will be no more death or sorrow or pain. The eager wait of creation for the revealing of the children of God will be over; creation will be free from bondage to decay and the groaning of labor pains will give way to a glorious birth (see Romans 8:19-25). And in the city the glory of God will be its light and the Lamb its lamp. "The nations will walk by its light and the kings of the earth will bring their glory into it" (Revelation 21:23-24). It will be a city filled with redeemed people and redeemed culture for the glory of God. And it will be our home forever.

Living Your Faith

1. In what ways do you tend to divide life into secular and sacred spheres?

2. How do you see your current or future vocation helping to fulfill God's redemptive purposes in the world?

3. List some elements of human culture that you think will be in the New Heaven and Earth.

Recommended Reading

The Call: Finding and Fulfilling the Central Purpose of Your Life by Os Guinness, Word.

Heaven Is Not My Home: Living in the Now of God's Creation by Paul Marshall, Word.

Redeeming Creation: The Biblical Basis for Environmental Stewardship by Fred Van Dyke et al., InterVarsity Press.

The Transforming Vision by J. Richard Middleton and Brian J. Walsh, InterVarsity Press.

fifteen

The Dangerous Call
Robbie Castleman

I DECIDED TO BECOME A NURSE BECAUSE I LOVED TO HELP MY DAD gut and clean rainbow trout. Looking at the little inflated lungs and figuring out what the fish ate last just fascinated me. In fact, nothing grossed me out—not fish, not the bloody noses of my friends, not anything needing stitches—so I figured I was cut out to be a nurse. The smell of really old people and my little sister throwing-up got to me, but I thought if I avoided geriatrics and pediatrics I'd be fine. And I was.

After graduating from nursing school, I worked for the most part in intensive care units for eighteen years. I liked the blood, guts and nonroutine of intensive care nursing, and I was good at it. But I wasn't called to be a nurse.

I decided to become a Bible teacher and got a whole new education to do that while I worked part-time in nursing. I love to teach the Scriptures. Nothing gives me more pleasure than to teach or lead a good Bible discussion. But I haven't been called to be a Bible teacher.

I haven't been called to be a wife either, but I am one. I haven't been called to be a mother, but I've done that too. I haven't been called to be a writer, but I'm a published author. I haven't been called to talk to a particular person, but I've led people to Christ by talking to them. So if I've not been "called" to any of these things, what does it mean to be "called"?

I am not called to be a nurse, Bible teacher, wife, mother, writer or evangelist. I am called by Jesus to follow him. Vocational choices are made by a called person, but the particularities of the work do not constitute my "call." This is an important distinction to make.

Confusion over Calling

The very problem with discipleship and vocation is seen clearly in the word *vocation* itself. *Vocation* in everyday language is usually used to indicate what work we do. The question is, how did *vocation* get so tightly identified with work? Well, I think it's because in our culture and time, we very often identify others and ourselves by what we do for work—our occupation. "What do you do?" is often the first question asked after being introduced to a new person.

The idea of "vocational choices" is pretty much a luxury of an affluent culture and a measure of democratic freedom. Most people over the centuries and in the world today don't get to make many choices. Not who to marry, where to live or what to do. The big decisions in life can be agonizing, but the freedom to choose is a manifestation of an economic, cultural and political situation that is for the most part positive. "Calling," however, is not mixed up in this vocational choice. People who have no freedom, no resources, no lifestyle options, no educational opportunities, people with nothing except a challenge to survive have been called to follow Jesus. Vocational choice can be an important part of exercising personal holiness, but it is not essential to our "calling" as Christians.

As Christians we might want to deny that "we are what we do," but in the emotional identification of our worth, we often feel this way. Our productivity, the health of the "bottom line" and personal professional growth are things by which we are measured (and that we use to measure ourselves), whether we are working for a law firm, managing a Burger King, teaching kindergarten or pastoring a church. Each of these can be what a person does occupationally, but they are not what constitute our essential "calling."

Rich Lamb points out in his book *Following Jesus in the "Real World"* that "the term *calling* in Scripture is never directly associated with a job or profession." In fact, if we thought more of who we are as called people, we would be less afraid to take personal and professional risks for the sake of the gospel in the workplace. If my identity is securely set in who I am in Christ, then I can make professional choices based on this and not on anything else.

This mixing up of what is vocation and what is work tends to rule out certain kinds of work as being truly worthy of a called person. Somehow we think God might value the work of a pastor over that of the Burger King manager. Why? Because *we* value "full-time Christian work" more than Burger King managers. And we end up with a kingdom full of people who feel "second class," not "called."

Hear This

There are two things essential to a calling: the caller who calls, and the hearer of the one who calls. *Vocation* has everything to do with a response of faith inseparable to obedience. We are called by God to follow Jesus. "Vocation" is who we are as disciples. We are called to follow Christ. And it is important that our first question about this call is *not* "So, how do I do this?" but "Who do I need to be in order to follow faithfully?" It's the difference between vocation and an occupation.

Disciples are called to be like Jesus, so that any choices we make—from whom to marry or what work to do—need to center more on Christ's character than our own desires. Jesus' character is rooted in his incarnation as fully God and fully human. In supreme humility he "did not regard equality with God as something to be exploited, but emptied himself, taking the form of a slave" (Philippians 2:6-7). In terms of vocational choice, then, it stands to reason that it should be a decision based on humility and not ambition. The questions asked about "what should I do with my life?" become more rooted in "how can I best serve?" rather than in "what do I want to do?"

This distinction is often most helpful in times when trying to decide between two or more work options. Sometimes the situation, compensation and job description are similar and sometimes not, but a choice has to be made. We often agonize over what it is that "God wants me to do."

When people have come to me for advice at such times and both options are legal, suitable for a disciple and seem fit for the person, my first response often is "Well, I don't think God really cares about which one you decide to do. I do think he has an interest in how each situation might influence your *call* to follow Christ." *An occupation needs to serve your vocation.* It's amazing how often the person making the decision has a clear idea how one is better for being a disciple than the other.

Finding the Best Jobs

Because I am called to be like Jesus, what is it that best uses my training, educational investment and talents to advance the honor of the gospel in this world? in this neighborhood? in this church? in this family? in this relationship? As a person *called*, how best do I say yes in following Jesus? If I know that what is central to the call is Jesus' call to *me*, then I am free to look at the options and ask the right questions that lead me to "seek first the kingdom."

What is God most concerned about? Personal holiness, the witness of faith communities, justice for the poor and oppressed, servant relationships, the benevolent care of creation, and the reconciliation of all peoples to each other and to Christ—to name just a few. These need to be the questions we ask when deciding on job or career, not just "What do I want to do?"

What's important about "vocational stewardship" is not so much "what" to do, but the "who" that you are. The "who" of Jesus in issuing the call and the "who" you are in being faithfully obedient to the call, these are the ingredients of a lifetime of discipleship.

Within the vocational life of a disciple there are occupational decisions to be made. People who know you well can often give sound advice in helping guide you to an occupation they can see you doing well and with satisfaction. Gift and asset-assessment tests or interviews can be helpful in identifying strengths and skills. A ready opportunity can sometimes be an indication of how best to use talents, gifts, education and other personal resources at a particular time. Prayer, especially with someone who cares about you, can help keep you "in line" with God's purposes and "in hearing distance" of God's direction. God often guides you through a small-group community of believers who share the journey with you. Saying yes to Jesus vocationally can mean a life of occupational hazards and risks. Following Jesus is the only secure way to live with "faith on the edge"!

Understanding vocation as a call to be a disciple following Jesus asks us to be vulnerable to his ideas, obedient to his agenda and willing to love God and our neighbors. Career options that are considered unconventional or costly become possibilities. Instead of setting up a law practice or medical practice in the suburbs, it's possible to practice rural medicine or law in the inner city. Instead of finding that your doctorate is getting you nowhere in higher education, you move to a country that needs your expertise, and you teach there. Instead of building a business-as-usual, you explore ways to train and use the often unemployable, like recovering addicts, repentant prisoners or unwed mothers.

"Who is my neighbor?" was a question that sought to set limits on the service of the questioner in Scripture. Sometimes when we ask, "What does God want me to do?" we are, in fact, trying to set limits on what we know through the Scriptures that he wants us to do. God's will for all our lives is very clear. Jesus said it was summed up in two commandments, "You shall love the Lord your God with all your heart, and with all your soul, and with all your mind . . . and you shall love your neighbor as yourself." In making decisions about work, one good question to ask is "What job might enable me to love the best?"

Here are some questions to consider when making decisions about work:
□ In the choices of vocation I have, how can I best love the Lord with all that I am and my neighbor to the extremes of how I would be loved?
□ How do I best give my life away to live the life I am called to live?
□ How can I best contribute to what counts in the kingdom?
□ How does this opportunity affect my commitment to my faith community? church? small group? spiritual mentor? those I serve? those who serve me?

Radical Priorities

I have a friend who graduated near the top of his class, passed the CPA exam the first time and was hired out of college by a prestigious accounting firm. Years later, he turned down a promotion because it would require him to be gone one weekend a month. He told his employers he couldn't do that because he had a prior three-year commitment to his church to serve as an elder and to be gone once a month would not honor that commitment. Too often, neither the business world nor the church sees kingdom priorities that clearly. Putting a cap on his career at that point was a more powerful witness to what it means to be called than anything else he could have done.

My husband and I have known people who have rented for a time before buying a permanent home in order to find their church home first. They wanted proximity to the church to facilitate their involvement in its life and community. These people have been far outnumbered by the families who never thought to ask kingdom questions about where they live or what work they do.

Another person who, while single, refused to ask salary questions until the final interview for a position. Knowing himself well, he knew how easy it was for a $50,000 starting salary to become "God's will" over the job that started at $20,000.

Scripture tells us that "you are not your own . . . you were bought with a price" (1 Corinthians 6:19-20). Because we are secure in belonging to God, we can risk everything to love God and others. The "vocational" bottom line in the kingdom is our call to follow Jesus into a life of sacrificial service. It's hard if not impossible to live a life of humility and servanthood when we aren't absolutely sure of who we are as called people. Even the service of Jesus was anchored in *who* he knew himself to be and not the task or service itself.

The prelude to Jesus washing his disciples' feet reads like this:

> Jesus, knowing that the Father had given all things into his hands, and that he had come from God and was going to God, got up from the table, took off his outer robe, and tied a towel around himself. Then he poured water into a basin and began to wash the disciples' feet and to wipe them with the towel that was tied around him. (John 13:3-5)

Knowing who he was and where he was going, Jesus did the work of the lowliest servant. Knowing *who he was* meant he could risk doing anything for the sake of love. And it's the same for us as his followers. Jesus told the disciples he washed their feet as an example for them to follow.

Be a person who is determined to count for the kingdom because you have been called by the King. Let the values of the King and his kingdom define the values manifest in what you "do for a living."

The Way Things Were Meant to Be

Work itself is a noble part of what it means to be human. The ordering and care of God's creation is good work given to the human family before the Fall. Productivity without competition or destruction, without want or waste, is impossible for us to imagine, but work was a perfect part of joy before the rebellion in Eden. After Genesis 3 all work became toil. Be clear about this: ever since the Fall, no job has ever been perfect. No job is perfectly satisfying or perfectly fit for who you are.

However, just like our relationship with God and with each other, the business of God's people is to make redemptive efforts that point to what work is designed to be. Our work, as God's called people, still needs to bring order out of chaos, light out of darkness and rightness out of wrong. There is no work within the parameters of Scripture that cannot be done by people called to love God and further his purposes in the world. A Burger King manager who seeks the kingdom by treating all employees with dignity and all customers with honesty is good for the neighborhood and can bring glory to God in the running of that business.

The top three reasons people who have kept the faith for over twenty years are making a difference in the world and living lives marked by the call of Christ are

□ *Convictions:* They were taught a worldview that was sufficient for the questions and crises of the next twenty years, particularly the challenge of modern consciousness with its implicit secularization and pluralization.

□ *Character:* They met a teacher who incarnated the worldview that they were coming to consciously identify as their own, and in and through that relationship they saw that is was possible to reside within that worldview themselves.

□ *Community:* They made choices over the years to live out their worldview in the company of mutually committed folk who provided a network of stimulation and support which showed that the ideas could be coherent across the whole of life.

from *The Fabric of Faithfulness* by Steve Garber, InterVarsity Press

The fruits of our work, from income to perks, are to be used to serve others. As called people we say yes to God because he has said yes to us. In order for our labor to contribute to the kingdom, the fruit of our labor from paychecks to public relations, from capital gains to profit sharing, from office space to the home we might buy, from groceries to days off, are submitted to the lordship of Christ. All of our labor and what comes from it needs to contribute to the "work of the Lord."

Some people asked Jesus, "What must we do to perform the works of God?" Jesus answered them, "This is the work of God, that you believe in him whom he has sent" (John 6:28-29). The work of believing that Jesus is the Son of God and the Savior of the world—that Jesus is God incarnate, who lived, died, rose, ascended and is coming again—is the work of kingdom people called by God to make that known in all we do. Called people, whatever you do, "put yourselves into it, as done for the Lord . . . since you know that from the Lord you will receive the inheritance as your reward; you serve the Lord Christ" (Colossians 3:23-24).

Living Your Faith

1. Describe how your occupation (the work you do or the work you are preparing to do) fits with your vocation (your call to be a disciple).

2. Ask two or three people who know you fairly well to summarize what they see as your gifts, talents and strengths. Then ask them how they could see you invest them (or more effectively invest them) for kingdom purposes.

3. Identify areas in your character that are the least/most Christlike where you work. Consider how your sense of call/vocation can make a difference in that place and with those you work with.

4. Think of someone who is in the process of a major occupational decision. How might you help them make that decision as a disciple?

Recommended Reading

The Call by Os Guinness, Baker.
Making Life Work by Bill Hybels, InterVarsity Press.

sixteen

Using Your Resources Wisely

Kevin Blue

IT'S YOUR MONEY AND YOU SHOULD DECIDE WHAT TO DO WITH IT."
"Of course you should own a car. You're an adult."
"It's no one else's business how you spend your money."

I have heard all of these things and many more regarding how I should think about money, finances and possessions. You may have noticed these messages in one form or another: a commercial here, a billboard there, a personal comment. Television, radio, friends, newspapers, magazines and family members tell us what to think about money and what we should do with it.

These three initial statements may be culturally true, but they are biblically false. I hadn't realized that fact until I began to explore the teaching of the Bible regarding money, wealth and possessions. The following are some lessons that God has helped me learn over the years.

Eternal Decisions

John Wesley, the key leader of the Methodist movement in England, recorded an experience that stirred me. He was living at Oxford and one evening found the maid at his door. It was a cold winter day, and he noticed that she only had thin clothing to wear. He resolved to give her some money for a coat, but he had little to offer. As a result, she went on her way with nothing. Wesley was saddened by his inability to give and felt convicted that the Lord was not pleased with how he had used his money. He had spent it needlessly on some thing he desired, and so he could not help one who God loved and had put in his path that day.

Wesley resolved to rethink and rework his finances. For the better part of his life he lived on the same amount of income that he began with. Though his income increased, he chose to keep his standard of living and his lifestyle at the original level. Biographer Charles White says Wesley believed that "with increasing income, the Christian's standard of giving should increase, not his standard of living." Just because he could afford things was no indication that he should purchase them. Rather, he lived simply, saved what he could have spent on luxuries and comforts for himself, and generously gave all that he had left over to meet the needs of those whose needs were real.

In Luke 16 Jesus tells a similar story. A rich man lived a luxurious life in the presence of a poor man who went hungry every day and had experienced extreme hardships. Both died and found that their fortunes in life were reversed in eternity. The rich man, due to his lack of compassion, found himself tormented in hell. Lazarus, the poor man, found himself comforted and without need in heaven. Even though the rich man cried out for mercy and asked that his family be warned, Jesus said that he and his family had all the instruction and warning that were necessary to make the right choice. There was no reversing the outcome once their lives were over.

Who Is Your Master?

Jesus taught that "no slave can serve two masters; for a slave will either hate the one and love the other, or be devoted to one and despise the other. You cannot serve God and wealth" (Luke 16:13).

Jesus then offers the story of the rich man and Lazarus as an object lesson of someone who has obviously served and loved money. In conversation we frequently use the word *serve* to mean that we are meeting someone's need. If a person serves someone, it means that she met his need. This is not what is meant in Luke. We cannot serve God in this sense. God has no needs (Psalm 50). He is self-sufficient, and as the old church mothers and fathers say, "He's God all by himself." He does not need us or any effort we might bring.

But there is another sense of the word *serve* in which *to serve* someone means *to obey* them. This is the language of slavery in biblical times. Slaves served (obeyed) their masters. This is very true of our relationship with God. In fact, the apostle Paul refers to himself as a slave of Christ. In doing so, he is saying that it is Christ's commands and guidance that he follows. From Jesus' teaching it is also apparently possible to obey money. However, it is not possible to obey both.

Now it is interesting that the passage does not tell us the rich man was consciously under the impression that he was obeying money. Many people deny that money is their master (or idol, since anything we hold more valuable than God is an idol). Yet when they have a couple of job offers, they find out which one offers more money and they take that one. When it comes to purchasing a car or house, dining out or going to the movies, the only real question is whether they can afford it. If the possibility of living an affluent lifestyle comes along (through gambling or a substantial inheritance), the question is not whether this is faithful but simply, Where do I sign up?

There is a clear test to find out whether we are people who serve God or money. It is this: Who makes decisions for us? If God had been the rich man's master in Jesus' story, the rich man would have helped Lazarus. Instead, his pursuit of wealth, comfort and luxury were obviously more important to him than God's commands. It got him one place—hell.

Western culture flaunts the values of consumerism, affluence and the pursuit of wealth with unabashed zeal. Advertisements on television tell us we should buy things to gain security or happiness or a beautiful mate. While these things may have been implied in the past, now they are stated overtly. The wealthy are honored more than the poor. Deference is paid to them. The broader culture encourages the accumulation of wealth because it provides a buffer against the harsh realities of the world. It is a doorway to pride. We think we are in control of life, instead of God. Any person who is truly a disciple of Christ must wrestle with this teaching and, by God's grace, grow into a person who does not live to pursue wealth as his or her aim in life.

Credit and Debt

Credit and debt plague many people today. Credit cards, educational loans, business loans and other financial entanglements are all part of the common fabric of our society. A person of faith, however, is interested in how to faithfully navigate this trend. Debt is a form of enslavement. It puts us in the position of not being free to give generously or to do the things God wants us to do. Currently, indebtedness threatens to undermine the fabric of society worldwide. A Christian should be wary of any type of indebtedness and should seek to avoid the purchases that incur it, especially unneeded purchases.

Live Simply

A disciple of Christ should seek to live a simple life. In teaching his disciples how to minister, Jesus "ordered them to take nothing for their journey except a staff; no bread, no bag, no money in their belts; but to wear sandals and not to put on two tunics" (Mark 6:8-9). And Luke 12:15 reads, "Take care! Be on your guard against all kinds of greed; for one's life does not consist in the abundance of possessions."

Some may hear this as a call to poverty. Jesus made this very call to one who desired to follow him but for whom materialism and the worship of money was the key barrier.

> As he [Jesus] was setting out on a journey, a man ran up and knelt before him, and asked him, "Good Teacher, what must I do to inherit eternal life?" Jesus said to him, "Why do you call me good? No one is good but God alone. You know the commandments: 'You shall not murder; . . .'" He said to him "Teacher, I have kept all these since my youth." Jesus looking at him, loved him and said, "You lack one thing; go, sell what you own, and give the money to the poor, and you will have treasure in heaven; then come, follow me." When he heard this, *he was shocked and went away grieving, for he had many possessions.* (Mark 10:17-22, emphasis added)

This is one of only two direct questions Jesus receives regarding the issue of eternal life. And it is one of two different direct responses he offers. He does not give this command to everyone he meets. However, though selling all we own is God's word to some of us, the real point is this: live simply. This is the road that a person of faith is called to travel on. Money is not ours, and we are not free to spend it on whatever we fancy. We are not *called* to buy a car or a house. Scripture clearly tells us that "the world and all that is in it" belongs to God (Psalm 50:12). As with everything we are given, we are *called* to use it as the King directs (Luke 19:11). We are no more free to spend our money any way we like than we are to have sex with anyone we encounter. It is shocking to think that when faced with the prospect of an eternal relationship with God, who promises to take care of us, many people would choose money or possessions instead.

One basic step in living simply is establishing some type of budget. If you have never tried to learn how to faithfully use the money and possessions that you have been entrusted with, it's okay. Any time is a good time to start to learn. The key is to learn and grow in this area.

A good first step in budgeting is to record how you spend your money for a month or two. Then take this information and evaluate whether, given the imperatives and values of the faith, you are being a wise or foolish steward of the resources God has given you. Good areas to take a hard look at would be entertainment (movies, videos, music, concerts) and dining out. These are areas of significant extravagance for many people. It is also worth considering whether any of us really *need* pagers, cell phones and virtual pets.

Some Practical Steps to Budgeting

Fast. Don't spend any money on entertainment, clothing or eating out for a month. Give the money you save to a charity or your church.

Credit. Resolve to charge no purchases until you pay off every current bill. Then pay your credit bill in full at the end of each month.

Loans. Take out as few loans as possible to finish your education. Examine other options to pay for tuition, such as working on campus or taking a little longer to finish your degree.

Giving

When creating a budget, consider the matter of giving different from the way you think about your other expenditures. Give first. Be more committed to giving than you are to spending money on anything else. The amount you give may not be greater, but be more committed to giving it. The tithe (the focus of much of today's teaching) is not really the standard of faithfulness in giving. It is more like the floor under which we will not go. Generous, joyous, free-spirited giving is the best thing we can do with our money and the best way we can use our stuff. Give so that others can receive the gospel and be discipled in the faith. Give so that others can have their basic needs met. Give so that you influence others to delight in God and so that people enter the kingdom with you (Luke 16:1-13).

One group of seniors and graduates of the University of Southern California decided to form a group that would give generously to see the work of sharing the gospel with others go forward at their campus. Numbering only seven to eight people, over several years they annually gave $20,000 to fund campus ministry there. There are many such possibilities and opportunities for giving if we are willing to seek them out and take advantage of them.

Accountability

It is helpful to let other people of faith know what you are doing with your money; ask their advice regarding your stewardship. If they love you, your finances are their business. In our fellowship when a person desires to make a purchase of more than $75, he or she will seek the counsel of two other fellowship members. We also regularly agree to open our financial accounts to one or two people in the group. These practices help us look closely at spending and lifestyle issues together. We are also hoping to share things like major appliances (washers, dryers, lawn mowers) rather than adhering to the cultural belief that each household should have one of these.

The power of money is one of the great forces in our world today. This is an issue of loyalty. God gives us use of things from time to time, through various means. But it is God alone who is the *owner*. We are the *owers*. It is by his Word and Spirit that any lifestyle choice must be considered. Simple living is the path that we should choose.

Living Your Faith

Several slogans that I have found helpful in remembering biblical principles regarding money and the stewardship of possessions are:

Things are to be used to serve people.

Enjoy giving generously and living simply.

Money should never make decisions for me.

People are more important than things.

1. How is your spiritual TEMPerature in regards to money and possessions? Which of the four principles can you put into practice this week?

2. How can you simplify your lifestyle and give more generously?

3. Are you currently in debt? What can you do to get out of debt as soon as possible?

Recommended Reading

Freedom of Simplicity by Richard Foster, Harper & Row.

Money & Power by Jacques Ellul, InterVarsity Press.

Rich Christians in an Age of Hunger by Ronald Sider, Word.

seventeen

Don't Worry,
There Is Time Enough
Bobby Gross

I NEVER SEEM TO HAVE ENOUGH TIME!" IS THIS YOUR LAMENT? IT'S often mine. We try to "find time" or "buy time" or "make time." We seem to "run out of time" so quickly, and while we "don't know where the time goes," we're pretty sure it "flies" there!

We in the industrialized, computerized West tend to live busy, fast-paced lives full of commitments and activities. We work hard, we play hard, and we are often pressured, tired and frustrated. We're not sure we'll ever catch up, much less get it all done. But we keep at it, muttering under our breath, "I wish I had more time."

I have a haunting suspicion that Jesus rarely, if ever, thought or lived this way. On the last night of his life, with a keen sense that the timing was right ("the hour has come"), Jesus makes a startling declaration in prayer: "I glorified you on earth by finishing the work that you gave me to do" (John 17:4). Jesus got it all done! He expresses a profound sense of completion and peace even though he faces death at thirty-something (an "early" death we would say). Undoubtedly there were times when Jesus worked hard and pushed himself (we know of at least two all-nighters), but I don't think Jesus struggled to "manage his time" as many of us do.

Jesus' example teaches us a bedrock truth: *there is time enough to do all that God wants us to do.* For me, this both convicts and encourages. It highlights that something is wrong when I continually "feel under the gun"—too much to do, too little time. But it also suggests that I need *not* live that way, at least not in order to please God. The bottom line: we *do* have enough time!

We tend to speak of time as a commodity or resource, as though it were ours to possess and use. But time neither belongs to us nor do we control it. Time is a *gift* from God. It is the dimension created by God for our very experience of life and being. Or simply put, time is not something we use so much as something we live within.

The real issue is not *time* management but *self*-management. We cannot manipulate time itself; we can only make choices about what we will do within it. We have been given a kind of *stewardship of time.* God has entrusted each of us with time, both the hours of each day and the years we will live. And with time he gives the responsibility to "manage" it by living our lives in line with his purposes. In this sense Jesus was a good steward of his time, and he wants to help us be good stewards of ours. Even more, to follow Jesus means to submit our use of time to his direction.

God at Work and Rest

"And on the seventh day God finished the work that he had done, and he rested on the seventh day. . . . So God blessed the seventh day and hallowed it" (Genesis 2:2-3). God reveals himself as one who works and one who rests. Likewise, as those created in his image we humans are designed and called to a rhythm of work and rest. We disregard this rhythm to our detriment.

When we work—and this includes study, volunteering, parenting, ministry—we fulfill one of the purposes God had for humanity from the start. We honor God by our work. Often, however, we overdo it. God provides patterns of rest as an antidote to our anxious toil. Sleep, sabbath and sabbatical are three gracious provisions that we need to take seriously.

Sleep. God made us to spend roughly a third of our lives asleep. Think about that for a moment. Why do we pull all-nighters or try to get by on as little sleep as possible? In order to get more done? God is not nearly as concerned about "maximizing productivity" as we often are. "It is in vain that you rise up early and go late to rest, eating the bread of anxious toil; for he gives sleep to his beloved" (Psalm 127:2). There is much grace hidden in the experience of sleep. It is a gift from God meant for our refreshment and benefit. Sleeping reminds us daily that we can only do so much, that ultimately *our* work is secondary to and dependent on *God's* ongoing work.

Here's good news: God has given us time for sleep. Make it your pattern to get the sleep you need (probably seven to eight hours a night) and you will enjoy not only physical and mental benefits but spiritual dividends as well.

Sabbath. If sleep is God's provision for rest on a daily basis, then sabbath is his provision on a weekly basis. "Remember the sabbath day, and keep it holy. Six days you shall labor and do all your work. But the seventh day is a sabbath to the LORD your God; you shall not do any work" (See Exodus 20:8-11). There are two ways to approach the fourth commandment. One emphasizes *law:* a day of restrictions, regulations and obligations. The other emphasizes *grace:* a day of provision and opportunity. Jesus highlights the grace angle: "The sabbath was made for humankind, and not humankind for the sabbath" (Mark 2:27).

Three priorities will help keep our sabbaths in line with God's intentions: *rest, reflection* and *relationship.* Sabbath should be a day of rest and restoration. This won't happen if the day is jammed with church commitments, household chores or taxing recreation. Slowing down allows room for reflection, for renewing spiritual identity, reviewing priorities, expressing thankfulness, contemplating creation and worshiping our Lord. Sabbath also offers time to nurture and enjoy relationships, foremost with our heavenly Father but also with family and friends. If these three themes shape our weekly sabbath, we will increasingly experience the day as a means of God's generous grace.

Don't be rigid about which day you observe. While most Christians observe Sunday, some will want to choose another day. Many students like to keep sabbath from sundown Saturday to sundown Sunday so that they can study on Sunday nights. Further, you will need to determine for yourself how to best rest, reflect and relate. The key is to be deliberate. It's all too easy to fill our day with less-than-sabbath activities, such as television or chores, and fail to do better things such as going for a walk, writing in our journals, making phone calls to friends or family, enjoying art or even taking a nap.

Sabbatical. A third provision for rest is the concept of sabbatical. Leviticus 25 describes how God called Israel to observe an extended sabbath, a whole year off from agricultural work in which God would provide for them. From this we can draw a broad sabbatical concept, namely, any extended time set apart for emotional rest and spiritual renewal. Variations of this practice range from a day of prayer to a three-day "retreat of solitude" to a purposefully designed vacation, to a full-fledged, six-to-twelve-month break from work or study. Think of Moses on the mountain or Jesus in the desert. God can accomplish deep and significant things through sabbatical experiences.

Tyranny of the Urgent

Your "to do" list is longer than your arm. Deadlines loom. You are always burning the midnight wattage. Dropped balls bounce at your feet. You find yourself apologizing for less-than-your-best work. Anxiety replaces joy, and your work or study is wearisome. Does this describe you?

In college I read *The Tyranny of the Urgent,* a booklet by Charles E. Hummel, and learned one of the fundamental problems of life management: "letting the urgent things crowd out the important." Urgent requests, deadlines, interruptions or crises can tyrannize us. And these pressures are most acute when we are over-committed.

Recently a Christian student at Columbia University apparently leaped to her death from the roof of a twenty-story dorm. No one will know the full story behind such a tragedy, but I was sobered to learn that she was vastly overextended in studies and campus activities. Sadly, the pressures resulting from trying to do more than time allowed may have contributed to her desperate act. Most of us are not suicidal, but some of us feel similar stress and anxiety.

Why do we take on so much or find it so hard to say no to the requests and expectations of others? Why are some of us so driven in our work or studies? If we dig below the surface of these behavioral patterns, we'll probably discover psychological and spiritual roots. We also may find plain-old ugly sin, such as idolatrous greed (the desire for wealth or fame or power), selfish ambition (the competitive instinct to exalt ourselves over others) or anxious insecurity (the determination to prove ourselves and gain the approval of our parents, peers or even God).

But Jesus wants us to learn *contentment* in lieu of greed, to develop *humility* rather than pride, and most profoundly, to receive *grace* in the face of our fears. His love for us does not depend on our worthiness or our work. Jesus tells the story of a landowner who hired idle day laborers to work in his vineyard for a fixed wage. Some started at 9:00 a.m., some at noon, some at 3:00 p.m. and some at 5:00 p.m. At quitting time, to the outrage of the "early birds," he paid everyone the same amount (Matthew 20:1-16). Likewise, God chooses to be generous to us; his love can be neither earned nor forfeited. Such grace is an antidote to our drivenness.

Making the Most of the Time

The apostle Paul urges, "Be careful then how you live, not as unwise people but as wise, making the most of the time, because the days are evil" (Ephesians 5:15-16). The context for this verse is Paul's call for believers to walk as "children of light" who try to find out what is pleasing to the Lord. We are to be deliberate in our choices and conscious of our opportunities. To be good stewards of our time, the two most important elements we need are *wisdom* and *discipline,* both gifts from God (James 1:5; 2 Timothy 1:7). It boils down to this: the wisdom to set right priorities and the discipline to act in light of them.

In Mark 1, after an exhausting day of ministry, Jesus rises before dawn to pray. This is where he gains wisdom and direction for the day's priorities and decisions. Thus he is able to resist the urgent demands of his closest friends and the ego-flattering expectations of the townsfolk. They want him to return to the village and multiply his impact. But he goes elsewhere. The need does not dictate his response. He has the discipline to say no to a good thing in order to choose the more important thing.

Yet Jesus was not bound by a rigid agenda or a tight schedule. In Mark 6 he has a clear goal of taking his disciples away to a deserted place to rest. But when they arrive at the spot, the crowds have anticipated his arrival and are waiting. Jesus has compassion and begins to teach them, laying aside for the moment his plan for a little R & R. After this full day of work Jesus sends his disciples ahead so he can be alone to pray. Time management, then, cannot be for us some regimented system that leaves no room for compassion or spontaneity or redirection from the Spirit of God.

Practical Tips and Tools

1. Set priorities and goals. Invest time in reflection and prayer, perhaps an evening each month or a day each semester. Write down the responsibilities, goals and relationships that should have priority in your life. Think about "being" as well as "doing" goals. Assess them for their degree of importance and urgency. Some will be *important-and-urgent,* some *important-but-not-urgent,* some *urgent-but-not-important* and some neither important nor urgent. Focus special attention on those that are important-but-not-urgent because these are the easiest to neglect. For example, investing time in a friendship or developing your creative potential are probably more important than spending hours watching television or surfing the web. Consider doing fewer things but with greater excellence.

2. Study your schedule. Picture this: you are ready to pack your car for vacation. Behind the open trunk sit suitcases, coolers, equipment and various bags. You start packing, perhaps ingeniously, but it soon becomes clear that it won't all fit. You must decide what to take and what to leave behind. Assess how you actually spend your time. Does it match up with your priorities and goals? Your list of goals, responsibilities and tasks is the luggage and your calendar is the trunk—and there's no roof rack! Put in the important things first, including time to plan, pray and rest.

3. Just say no! How should you respond to interruptions, requests and new opportunities? Often you will simply say no because your priorities are set and your schedule is full. You will resist the urgent to protect the important. Usually you are *not* the only one who could do a given thing, nor must it be done immediately. If the request has merit, you will always ask for time to prayerfully think about it; you rarely decide on the spot.

"When do you need a response from me by?" has been a lifesaver from saying yes to things that look great at the moment but lose their sheen after a few days of reflection and prayer. And when you do say yes, you must consciously decide what you will "take out of the trunk" to make room for this new item. This is why it's good to leave "margins" in our lives and schedules.

4. Seek advice and accountability. Ask a mature friend, a peer you respect or your small group to help you evaluate your priorities, schedule and use of time. A mentor or accountability partner can add great wisdom to your thinking and help reinforce your self-discipline. And maybe you could return the favor!

5. Utilize tools. There are many planning systems available to enhance time management. I've found three tools to be essential. First, I keep written lists of responsibilities and goals, a broad one for the whole year or semester and a more specific one for each month. On each list I prioritize the items with an *A, B* or *C* (*A* means important or primary). Second, I use a calendar book that allows me to look at a month's schedule on one page and that contains schedule pages for each day. I can see the big picture— upcoming deadlines, travel, events—as well as mark down appointments and block time for each day's tasks. Third, I use "to do" lists. Again I have a weekly list, divided into two columns by priority, and a daily list. Using these simple tools together with the habit of regular prayerful review and planning can enable you to make the most of your time.

The Time Beyond Time

The writer of the book of Hebrews speaks of salvation and the experience of the new heaven and earth as a kind of ultimate sabbath: "So then, a sabbath rest still remains for the people of God" (see Hebrews 4:9-11). We are destined for an existence that God describes as eternal. In that realm we will not struggle to manage our time but will enjoy an unimaginable freedom to do our work and offer our worship as part of the eternal rest that we will share with our Creator and Redeemer. This is our great hope. Meanwhile, as we seek to be faithful stewards of our lives, we have this promise of grace from Jesus: "Come to me, all you that are weary and are carrying heavy burdens, and I will give you rest" (Matthew 11:28).

Living Your Faith

1. Do you tend to get overextended? Why? Why is it so hard to say no?

2. What disciplines of rest—sleep, sabbath, sabbatical—do you need to implement or strengthen in your life?

3. What disciplines of self-management—prayer, planning, saying no—do you need to learn or sharpen?

Recommended Reading

Freedom from Tyranny of the Urgent by Charles Hummel, InterVarsity Press.

Keeping the Sabbath Wholly by Marva J. Dawn, Eerdmans.

Margins: How to Create the Emotional, Physical, Financial & Time Reserves You Need and *The Overload Syndrome: Learning to Live Within Your Limits* by Richard Swenson, both NavPress.

eighteen

Compassion for the Poor
Kevin Blue

DRIVING TO WORK ALONG THE STREETS OF LOS ANGELES, I WAS stopped by a red light. A man stepped off the curb and began to meander in and out between the cars, asking people for change. He was dressed in rags and hadn't washed in a while. He placed his hands together like a child first learning to pray and at times he knelt to ask for help. Most drivers didn't roll their windows down. Few even looked at the man. They continued to look straight ahead, pretending he wasn't there. The light turned green before he got to me, and people raced off, barely allowing him to make it to the sidewalk. He began to walk back to the corner where his routine would begin again.

This is a common sight these days. At work when walking anywhere, I am approached at least once for change. After a while this gets to be a little much. I have found myself looking ahead and sometimes taking a different route just so I don't have to deal with these people. I have found my love lacking.

Two Bikes and a Rake

One morning I woke up late. It was cold and rainy out, and as I rushed to get
ready, the doorbell rang. It was Ron. I had known him for about two years, during which he had become poorer as he developed a drug habit. He had done
some yard work for us in the past and often washed cars for food and money.

Once I bought him a bus ticket so he could get back to his family in another
part of the country and get back on his feet. I didn't see him for a few months.
Now he was back in town, looking for help again. Though nearly late for a
meeting, I heeded the counsel of Scripture to do unto others as you would have
them do unto you. I let him in and had him take off his wet jacket and sit by the
heater. I fixed him a hot breakfast, put it in front of him and went to take a
shower. I was in the bathroom for about ten minutes. When I came out, the
plate was clean, the front door open and my bike and Ron had disappeared.

Later that night he came back and, having unlocked a side window during
his previous visit, stole another housemate's bike. I never saw him again.

When I first began seeing God's love for the poor in Scripture, caring for
them was both a novel idea and an exciting adventure. But to be honest, it
quickly lost much of the glamor. I found some poor people very demanding, ungrateful and belligerent. I have had two bicycles and various garden-
ing tools stolen from my house. Sometimes I laugh when I tell these stories, but they were not so funny when they happened. So the Scriptures
look a little different to me now. I read them with a better understanding of
the *cost* of love. But it's funny; despite my more realistic view of what it
means to love the poor, I come up with the same thing: God calls me to
have compassion on ("suffer with") those in need.

The Lord hears the cry of the poor. Blessed be the Lord. Love for those
in need is not optional; it is a central mandate of the faith. It's not a political
issue; it's a biblical one. It's so much at the heart of who Jesus is, so much
a part of his character, that he tells us if we do not love those in need, we do
not love him. Loving the poor is one of the clear marks of a disciple,
regardless of how we are treated in return.

Serving Them Is Serving Him

Matthew 25:31-46 tells us that when Jesus returns to earth and separates the righteous from the unrighteous, he will reward those who have been faithful to him with eternal blessing and joy in the presence of the Father. He will also punish those who have been unfaithful by exiling them to eternal punishment apart from God. The baseline that the Lord uses to render his judgment is "Did you have compassion on those in need?" It is the one deciding issue. In fact, Jesus so identifies with the needy that our treatment of them becomes our treatment of him. In Luke 10:25-37 he tells us that having eternal life involves showing practical love to the needy. In Luke 7:20-23 Jesus' care for the poor serves as his messianic credential. Love for the poor is a sign and wonder that witnesses to the power of God among people (Luke 4:18, 7:22).

One litmus test of our love for God is not just sympathy toward the poor but a lifestyle of love and service to those in need. One shocking example comes from the book of Amos. In Amos 5:23-24 God says he hates religious gatherings and songs of praise when they are without substantive commitments to justice and righteousness. Our worship services and fellowship gatherings, our singing and playing of musical instruments, are not only worthless in the absence of justice and righteousness, they even incite God to anger. In worship we claim to respect and honor God and his Word, praising him for his character and pledging our faithfulness. Yet if we refuse to actually take his Word seriously by caring for the poor, our worship mocks God.

A Man of Modest Means

Jesus' life offers a clear testimony that God identifies with and has compassion on the poor. Jesus was born to two very common people, in a stable with smelly barn animals around. He was laid in a manger, the animal feeding trough being full of straw and, perhaps, barnyard slobber. His was a blue-collar family, the father working with his hands as a carpenter. The city of Jesus' birth, Bethlehem, was nothing special—full of common people just like his family. It was a poor man's birth.

Jesus had a common, everyday name (like John in the United States or Maria in Mexico). He grew up in Nazareth, a small city with a poor reputation. People looked down on folks from this area of the country. According to custom, Jesus would have learned the trade of his father, becoming a carpenter. This means he was strong, "cut," you might say, from hard and heavy work, before he began his ministry.

Jesus' disciples were a bunch of no-names. They had a minimal education. There were violent, politically subversive and generally rowdy people among his closest followers. Jesus' audience largely consisted of the sick, the lame, the blind, lepers, prostitutes and the poor. They were the common people of cities and rural areas.

During his public ministry, Jesus lived as a homeless person (Matthew 8:20). He had no apparent source of income other than the generosity of those who followed him. There is no evidence that he had any property or material possessions to speak of, save the clothes that he wore. He lived the way he called his disciples to live when he sent them out. By all accounts this would be the life of a person who is relatively poor. He was not starving or diseased, but he possessed nothing that would identify him as either middle class or wealthy.

A More Precise Message

Many impoverished or oppressed people have a strong need to know that God will provide for them in such a way that they don't have to remain poor. Saying that Jesus was poor threatens their acutely felt need for financial stability and provision. It is as though they were taught that "Jesus was poor, and therefore you should be happy to be poor. You should not worry about health care or going hungry on occasion. Be satisfied with what you have. It may be unjust, but because Jesus was poor, you should be happy with that."

This is not the teaching of the Bible. The intent of the kingdom is neither to keep some people poor nor to make all believers rich, but rather to see that everyone's needs are met. Christian disciples are called to care for those in need, and there is no possibility of knowing God or finding favor with him apart from practical compassion for those in need.

Though a strong case can be made against isolating the poor, the reality of many neighborhoods is that they are already divided by economic class. A biblical and wise alternative is for wealthier people to relocate into poorer areas. This alternative often raises many objections: What about my safety, the safety of my family, the education of my kids? The list goes on. But it was the life that Jesus chose to live, and since we are called to "walk

as he walked," it would be wise for us to consider this type of action.
Rather than allowing fear, difficulty and possible suffering decide for us,
and rather than having comfort and affluence lure us, faithfulness to God
must guide the disciple's choices.

Getting Practical

A newlywed couple relocated to a poor neighborhood in response to this teaching. A wave of burglaries had swept through the neighborhood in the previous
months. A few months after my friends moved in, they were burglarized. Many
of their wedding gifts and other valuables were taken while they were at work.
They felt threatened, vulnerable and violated. They were afraid, experienced
periodic waves of extreme insecurity and debated whether or not they should
move. After some discussion and prayer, they decided to stay. Having their
stuff stolen was part of what it meant to suffer with their neighbors. It was part
of what it meant to incarnate the gospel there among their neighbors.

In the long run their willingness to stay and endure evil (just like Jesus)
became the decisive event used by God to build trust with neighbors. It was
the beginning of beautiful relationships. Neighbors began to look out for
each other, and one young woman found faith in Jesus.

Many believers have had to endure even more difficult trials. But their
witness is the same. God calls Christians to associate with the needy and
bear the same burdens that they do, enduring the same problems, pains and
joys of their lives—just as Jesus did.

Some of us, for kingdom-oriented reasons, will choose to not "go with
the flow" of our culture's tendency to live better and acquire even more. For
example:

☐ A group of college students decided to put their finances together to help
support the education and physical needs of a child in another country.

☐ A local church helped organize various neighbors to close down a liquor
store that was a destructive force in their area.

☐ Several suburban churches volunteer time and practical skills to help
develop a neighborhood ministry in a poor neighborhood. They give financially, and many of the people who have been involved have built relationships with people who are a part of that local ministry.

□ A woman heard her company was upgrading its computers and asked that the old models be donated to a youth ministry for kids in a poorer neighborhood. This ministry seeks to empower children and their families by serving their educational needs.

□ One church has developed a ministry to homeless men that feeds them and helps them clean up, find jobs and get housing. It also offers them the good news of Christ.

□ Several college fellowships have chosen to help students pursue summer mission opportunities among the poor in the United States and abroad.

Choosing one of these options is not as important as being creative, praying about how you might respond to this word from God and cooperating with him as he gives you opportunities and ideas to act on.

If we follow Jesus, our packed schedules and our fears and misgivings must not dissuade us from having compassion for the poor. We must, with the Lord's help, become people of courage who actually follow God into this kind of life. When I'm intentionally following another car and it turns right, I turn right. For some of us, following Jesus into a compassionate life will mean making a U-turn. Let's not be fainthearted in making the turn. There is a life of blessing and intimacy with God that awaits those who follow him. We must pray for the faith and courage we need to move forward. It doesn't matter what you have or how much you make. Rather, what matters is that your resources are used not only to provide for yourself, your family and God's people but also those in need.

Living Your Faith

1. Have you ever been taken advantage of by someone in need? How did it make you feel?

2. How might your life mirror Jesus' life?

3. How will you care practically and compassionately for those in need?

4. Are there other Christians around you who you can join in this service?

Recommended Reading

Beyond Charity by John Perkins, Baker.
Rich Christians in an Age of Hunger by Ronald Sider, Word.

nineteen

Loving Justice
Paul Tokunaga

THIS SUSHI IS TO DIE FOR!"

"That dress is to die for!"

"The BMW Z3—now that's a car to die for!"

"To die for"—that's how the apostle John's description of the
New Heaven and the New Earth makes me feel—far *more* than for sushi,
dresses and Z's. *Far more.*

To die—and then live forever in a place with no more drive-by shoot-
ings, no more folk without homes, no more neighbor sending us unwar-
ranted, threatening letters and phone calls, would be—heavenly. We've gotten so used to a sin-full world that it's hard to imagine fairness, rightness,
straightness, truthfulness and integrity being commonplace.

This is not wishful thinking or a passing fancy. It is a dream come true.
Life now is *not* as good as it gets. For some of us it is going to get better,
much better.

The Biblical Vision: Being Signposts of the Ultimate "Straightness"
The Lord Jesus gave John a sneak preview of heaven. John then recorded it

for us in the last two chapters (21 and 22) of Revelation. His word-pictures capture purity, breathtaking beauty and great relationships devoid of jealousy, one-upmanship and competition. We will *finally* love others with a depth and passion equal to how Jesus has always loved us.

Why should we "do justice"?

The first of three reasons is: *We struggle for justice in the here and now because it points to the "there and later."*

John's picture of the New Heaven and the New Earth has compelled me to march for "just causes," boycott unethical companies, write and speak out against racism, and write articles for the campus newspaper that called into question unethical practices which harmed people. With John's picture in mind, I gave money to support a child in Uganda and to send lobbyists to Washington D.C. who rally support for policies that free up food for the impoverished.

"See, I am making all things new." . . . Then he [God] said to me, "It is done! I am the Alpha and the Omega, the beginning and the end. To the thirsty I will give water as a gift from the spring of the water of life. Those who conquer will inherit these things, and I will be their God and they will be my children." (Revelation 21:5-7)

The New Testament connects human history with the New Heaven and New Earth. Paul describes God's cosmic plan of redemption in Colossians 1:15-20. There he explains that God intends to restore all things, whether in heaven or on earth, in other words, everything in the created order, to its intended *wholeness.*

For me this is the most compelling argument to "do justice." When he said to the Father, "Your will be done, *on earth as it is in heaven,*" Jesus' prayer was also a call for us to do "heavenly things" right now, right here. The Hebrew root word for justice is almost synonymous with "righteousness" or "straightness." When we do "just things," we demonstrate the rightness and straightness that the New Heaven and the New Earth will fully embody.

Our Hearts Should Resemble His Heart for This Planet and Its People
Second, because God's own heart beats so strongly for justice, so should ours. He created this world with rhyme and reason. When Adam and Eve

chose to listen to a voice other than God's, it set in motion a rebellion against Creator and creation that has been going strong for thousands of years. That rebellion has brought famine, widespread poverty, natural and unnatural catastrophes, destructive wars and horrid acts of violence.

Our Creator is no aloof deity. He is no celestial clock maker constructing a great machine and letting it tick away unattended while he starts new ventures with other universes and planets. He ups the ante for those who say they belong to him but don't act like responsible family members. He hates it when we "do church" but don't have justice and mercy flowing from our lives (Amos 5:21-24).

When our "faith on the edge" compels us to think and feel more like Jesus, we will not read front-page stories about rape in our cities or watch the horrible headline news about the annihilation of innocent people in Kosovo or Colorado. Nor will we drive through ravaged neighborhoods with nonchalance or disdain. When God's heart breaks for the falleness of his creation, so will ours.

Those who follow Jesus are key players in God's reclamation project. When we "do justice," we are both getting people ready for the *future kingdom* and reflecting God's heart and values into the *present world*. What an enormous task and wonderful privilege!

How we spend our time and resources *now* does matter. We're to ask that worn but dead-on-target question, "What would Jesus do?" Asking that question in regard to the choices before us and then daring to follow his voice will transform the world and us. When we choose to follow him, paths to incredible places will begin opening up before us.

Last May, Ivy graduated from Harvard and was accepted into a top-notch medical school. She decided to step out for a year of missions work before starting her med program.

She spent the first three months as part of a missionary team serving small Honduran villages. Hurricane Mitch hit Honduras with full force, killing thousands and essentially shutting down the country.

For the weeks following, Ivy and her coworkers went from village to village with medical aid. Ivy e-mailed her friends and church family, "Many of you have asked me about the emotional and spiritual toll of seeing such tragedy. I think living in the middle of it has been better for my faith than if I had only

seen it on CNN. Here I am witnessing true faith, and it is contagious. I have been experiencing a period of renewal in simple faith. God is good and He loves his people. The faith of the Honduran people has blessed me."

Tomorrow, Ivy leaves for Guatemala City, where she will work with a ministry that serves the three thousand people who live in and make their living from the city's garbage dump. They are considered Guatemala's untouchable caste. Ivy will live three blocks from the dump, and the ministry's center is right next to the dump, "the most dangerous region in the city."

I'm convinced Ivy will never be the same after this year "off" in Honduras and Guatemala. She will be a different kind of doctor, I'm sure. Her compassion has deepened. Her faith has been stretched. A year ago, when a family in our church (we attend the same one as Ivy's family) lost four of five members in a plane crash in Guam, Ivy's faith was challenged. "How could God let this happen to this vibrant Christian family?"

My heart was touched when I read in Ivy's e-mail: "There was an undeniable presence of God in my life. The timing of everything was like God pulled out his planner and jotted down every event. I feel like He answered my prayers and made His presence clear because of His grace towards me, my lack of faith, and my need for evidence."

She ends it with: *"Todo lo puedo en Cristo que me fortalece"* ("I can do all things through Christ who strengthens me") (Philippians 4:13).

Evangelism and Justice Go Together

Third, we "do justice" because it authenticates our verbal proclamation that Jesus loves everyone. Christians regularly get raked over the coals for talking a good game but living a poor one. Evangelism and doing justice go together: evangelism points people to God, and doing justice demonstrates his care for them.

The person who builds a house for the poor and the person who explains saving faith in Jesus to the new owner are often one and the same. Ivy's e-mail recounted the power of the gospel when it was accompanied with helping those in need.

God-Values

As we study the Scriptures God clearly shows us his "values" woven throughout the Book.

God extends extra care for those marginalized by their society and left voiceless. His roll call includes widows, orphans, racial outcasts, the poor, the unborn, those politically oppressed, those with physical ailments. He urges his people to demonstrate care for them (Exodus 23:9; Luke 19:1-10).

God judges evil. He judges evil and metes out punishment. The Old Testament book of Habakkuk helps us understand how he does it. Habakkuk complains about how God seems silent and powerless while violence, injustice and wickedness apparently reigns. God answers by saying that he works through corrupt kings and powers to accomplish his purposes. He tells Habakkuk in the midst of such violence and destruction, "the righteous live by their faith" (Habakkuk 2:4).

God's justice includes economic solutions. In the Old Testament, especially in Deuteronomy, God prescribes measures for the Jewish community that levels the playing field so the rich don't get too rich and the poor don't suffer needlessly at their expense (Deuteronomy 24:10-15; Psalm 9:7-12).

In the New Testament his care continues. Sharing of possessions marked the first Christian "community" (Acts 2:44-47). His leaders curb a disparity brought on by racial differences (Acts 6:1). Wealthy congregations, like those at Antioch, helped others in financial difficulty (Acts 11:27-30).

Jesus: The God who looks like us. Jesus interacted with a huge variety of folk. For starters: a crooked tax collector, a woman caught with someone else's husband, merchants selling wares in the wrong venues, a high-ranking official of the despised Roman military, hypocritical religious leaders, unethical lawyers, an extortionist, slaves, social outcasts, wealthy rulers and a hungry crowd numbering well over five thousand. As he interacts with them, we see qualities deeply rooted in the character of God. When a shouting down is called for, Jesus booms forth. Similarly, he seethes with rage as he makes a whip to lash out at greedy merchants.

There's another side to Jesus' "rightness." With Zacchaeus, who made his millions defrauding innocent people, Jesus adroitly invited himself to stay in the man's home. He didn't sprint from sinners. And Zacchaeus was changed!

No single encounter gives us a complete picture of God's heart for justice, but a careful reading of any of the Gospels shows us God incarnate *doing the right thing again and again.*

Taking Baby Steps to Reflect God's Heart

As summer editor of our college newspaper, I joined forces with our left-wing student-body president to put on a blood drive for two young hemophiliacs. I didn't agree with all his politics and he didn't buy my Christianity, but we shared concern that these two guys would get the blood they needed.

My parents were imprisoned, along with 120,000 other Japanese Americans, in concentration camps during World War II. Because the pain was so deep, it was too difficult for them to talk about the experience. In college I began to speak on their behalf to various groups.

Learning about what happened to them helped me to see how other ethnic minorities have often been treated unfairly. I saw how Mexican American farm workers were being underpaid. I got involved in the United Farm Workers' iceberg lettuce and grape boycott in southern California because I knew God wanted those migrant farm workers paid fairly—and so should I.

Reading *The Autobiography of Malcolm X* by Alex Haley opened my eyes to African Americans. We moved to the Southeast twenty-one years ago in part to try to play some small role in reconciliation between blacks and whites.

In recent years I helped start the Southeast chapter of the Japanese American Citizens League, a social and civil rights organization. I did it in part because of the increasing number of hate crimes being committed against Asian Americans.

Gittin' Goin'

Old Chinese proverb: "The journey of a thousand miles begins with the first step."

Gittin' goin' is often the hardest part, but it doesn't have to be. Remember when you first tried swimming? Your goal was not to have the form of an Olympic champion. You weren't even embarrassed about those water wings on your arms. You just didn't want to drown.

Just git goin'. Here are some suggestions:

☐ Pick up a study guide like *Loving Justice* (IVP) by Bob and Carol Hunter or any of the guides in the Global Issues series (IVP). Find a friend to do the study with.

☐ Your study will give you a sense of God's heart for justice. What areas of need are you naturally drawn to?

☐ Who or what agencies are already doing what you feel drawn to? (This is usually a better option than starting your own agency, at least when you're just gittin' goin'.)

☐ Find out what justice involvement(s) your fellowship or church might already be committed to.

☐ It usually works best to get involved with your friends. There are lots of side benefits of getting involved with fellow believers: it gets you more involved in the fellowship or church; you can hold each other accountable for your commitment to the task; you get to see your friends more often; it makes your group Bible study or the pastor's sermons more relevant when several of you can apply the lesson to the same task.

☐ If you're a student, start by checking out the student activities office that sounds something like "Community Service" or "Volunteer Services."

☐ If you're not a student, try the United Way or look up "Social Service Organizations" in the Yellow Pages.

☐ Pick up the phone and make that first call.

Common Potholes When Desiring to "Do Justice"

Alienating your friends. Once you have embraced a cause and feel like it is God's will for you to be involved, it's easy to assume that it's God's will for all of your friends in your fellowship or church. Wonder why they turn the other way when you approach? Chances are you've become a one-note melody, and people have other notes in their lives. A good remedy: remember what you were like a year before you started "doing justice."

The need for balance and grace. If you aren't balanced, burnout will come. If you don't give grace to those who don't approach it as you do, you will become disillusioned and grow bitter ("Don't they see how important this is?").

My views/approach/theological position is right, so obviously yours is wrong—another good friendship killer. "Justice issues" are rarely simple, cut and dried. There's a lot more gray area than meets the eye. Ask God to give you grace to respect others' views, especially if they are people with whom you want to continue having a relationship.

Love your "enemies" instead of demonizing them. When you have a "holy cause," keep in mind Jesus died for those who might oppose you.

Change must come—now! The issue you and others in your fellowship or church are working on did not begin last week. It took a long time to become what it is today, and it will take a long time to cure, resolve, fix or dismantle. Recognize God's timetable is often different from ours (usually slower). The title of Eugene Peterson's wonderful book *A Long Obedience in the Same Direction* says it well.

Your views might change. Over months and years your views on this most important area of your life may change. Or the fires of your once-flaming passion may become embers. *Change* in involvement in a cause or mission is often more difficult than changing jobs or even careers. That mission represented who you were at the core of your being. Know that it won't be easy to leave. Give yourself grace. Talk it through with a fairly objective third party. Pray a lot. Don't let your mind discard all the good you did.

To Die For?

Winston Churchill rose to address the graduating class of Sandhurst, Great Britain's equivalent to the U.S.'s West Point. It was his alma mater. It was during World War II when his nation leaned heavily on Churchill, its prime minister, for leadership. On his shoulders was the task of inspiring his nation to a cause "to die for."

"Never ("nevah" is more accurate) give up."

He lowered his voice. *"Nevah* give up."

Then he raised it: "Nevah . . . Give . . . Up!"

He sat down.

Living Your Faith

1. As part of your regular study of Scripture, keep in mind these kinds of questions:

☐ What kinds of people seem to catch the brunt of God's warnings and admonitions?

□ What kinds of people seem to be recipients of his care and concern more than usual?

□ What things aggravate God and "get his goat"? What kinds of things upset him?

2. Dare to ask some very contemporary questions as you study the Scriptures. Such as:

□ In what ways does God come off like a Republican? A Democrat? A Socialist? Which party's current agenda do his values best line up with?

□ Is God supportive or opposed to affirmative action?

□ Why aren't there more _____ (name a specific ethnic or socially marginalized group) in our church or fellowship?

□ How would Jesus have counseled a thirteen-year-old poor, pregnant, unwed girl about her options?

Recommended Reading

Global Issues Bible Study series (9 study guides), InterVarsity Press.

Good News About Injustice by Gary A. Haugen, InterVarsity Press.

Loving Justice (LifeGuide Bible Study) by Bob and Carol Hunter, InterVarsity Press.

Theirs Is the Kingdom by Bob Lupton, Harper & Row.

A Theology As Big As the City by Ray Bakke, InterVarsity Press.

twenty

Evangelism: Going, Staying, Blessing, Telling
Jonathan Tran

I DON'T HAVE THE GIFT OF EVANGELISM. PEOPLE AREN'T DROPPING like flies into the kingdom all around me. The Holy Spirit doesn't spontaneously instruct me about when and with whom to share the gospel. I haven't come up with a unifying theory that amalgamates fifty-two different techniques of evangelism into one unstoppable, unbeatable method for converting people. I don't even like the word *evangelism* because I have seen plenty of bad evangelism.

But I have many non-Christian friends. I have a whole family that does not know Jesus. Everyday I interact with dozens of people who do not have a relationship with Jesus. They seem happy, but I know there is little joy without God. This bothers me. And so I evangelize.

Evangelism isn't a gift thing; it's a gospel thing. Too often we excuse ourselves from the work of evangelism because we do not have the gift of evangelism. We assume that gifted evangelists would not feel fear or uneasy or awkward like we do. So we leave the task to others who have better techniques or who do not get scared.

God has called us to the work of evangelism because he cares about people. We should be grasped by the gospel, for it is the power of God unto salvation for all who believe. Our world, our friends, are suffering; their lives are not okay without Jesus. We need to be concerned that so many are headed for hell. But God left us on this earth and put us in our classes and offices for a reason. God desires that none should perish—none of our classmates and none of our coworkers. Do we understand that? God wants *none* to perish.

This is an amazing thing about our God—that even as the world has committed unspeakable adultery against him, he still wants people back. We ought to be grasped by that in all of its absurd, ironic majesty. When we are, when we have just a small piece of God's heart for people, then we will become one of the most powerful, life-changing forces at our schools and workplaces.

I want to give you some principles for evangelism. This is not a technique that will make sharing Jesus easier. Evangelism is a long-haul work where you enter into someone's world and lay your life down for him or her. It is not easier nor harder than that.

Going

People have broken relationship with God. By going into people's worlds, God is restoring relationship. For the most part people are not going to come to us. We can have the most effective seeker-sensitive, gospel-enriched, inoffensive Christian activities, yet apart from deep relationships where we go across boundaries, most people will not go to God. It's not about our music, our clothes, our message bracelets. It's how we go out of our way to embrace folks who are fundamentally different. The gospel message has an inherent call: go.

Jesus crossed boundaries into unfamiliar, scary, ugly places. The whole God-to-human boundary was quite a divide. Jesus did go from almighty, glorious God to helpless child born in a barn, where animals eat, mate and defecate in the same place (an appropriate metaphor for our world). He went from worshiped Creator to rejected heretic, for his own neither knew him nor received him. He went from fellowshipping with the Father and the Spirit to relating with the man with two thousand demons and the woman who had five husbands. He went from being ministered to by the angels to ministering to a woman who had a twelve-year menstruating period, to a man who sold out his own people. He went from being called *Prince of Peace* to being called *the devil,* from *Sufficient* and *Faithful* to *drunkard* and *glutton.* Then he went to the Cross. Jesus was all about going. He went to you.

When Steve was a junior, he was living in a nice, comfortable, quiet, inexpensive apartment off-campus. He enjoyed the many creature comforts that came with having his own place. The next year Steve moved back into the dorms to spend more time with non-Christians. He was the only senior living in that hall. At this public university it was unheard of for seniors to live in the dorms. The dorms were ugly, uncomfortable, loud, 11' X 11' and absurdly expensive. But Steve decided to go into the world of those fifty freshmen.

DeeDee works with a popular car insurance firm. Many people know she is a Christian. DeeDee enters into the worlds of her coworkers. She comes to after-hours office parties and spends time in bars with them. DeeDee breaks their stereotypes of Christians who judge and condemn the secular social world. DeeDee's going into this world has produced great trust from her friends.

Staying

After you go somewhere and you find out it's a difficult place to be, an uncomfortable relationship to stay in, an unfamiliar setting with unfamiliar rules, you might feel tempted to go back to where you came from. After all, who wants to be in a place that feels weird and strange?

Going is hard. Staying is harder. For those on secular campuses or in secular jobs, it is a strong temptation to commit most of our free time to safe, comfortable relationships with Christians. We have a few friendships with nonbelievers and go to some of the places they go, but as soon as things get a little uncomfortable, we leave. The type of love Jesus is calling us to necessitates that we stay in relationships even when discomfort sets in.

Jesus didn't leave. He didn't leave when the demoniac threw a demon tantrum or when the leper ran up and touched him. He didn't leave when he started feeling sad for the widow at Nain or when religious leaders hated him. He didn't leave when followers misunderstood him or when the disciples were faithless, again and again. Jesus crossed boundaries and stayed with people who were uncomfortable to be with. He stayed with tax collectors and "sinners." He stayed with the fighting sisters Mary and Martha, and, amazingly, he stayed on the cross. At any point Jesus could have said, "That's it. I'm through with you people, you hard-hearted, idol-worshiping, wrong-religion-following, unbelieving people! I'm going to go back to the Trinity compound where I'm known, understood and celebrated. I'm outta here." Instead, he stayed. When things got uncomfortable and scary, he hunkered down and stayed with people. He stayed with you.

When Steve started dipping into savings to pay for his dorm room and his grades dropped as he gave his life away to the freshmen, he stayed. When DeeDee found her faith the butt of jokes, she didn't leave. Steve and DeeDee didn't leave because they knew that their friends needed Jesus.

Once we get over the need to be comfortable, we can start being people who stay. We see people through the good and the bad. We learn to enjoy them and care for them. People get to see us through our good and bad. They learn to enjoy us and care for us. It is these long-haul relationships that afford the most room for the gospel to articulate all of its grace and truth.

Blessing

Jesus was really good news for people. In Luke 4, commencing his ministry, standing up in a crowded church and reading from the prophet Isaiah, Jesus proclaims about himself:

> The Spirit of the Lord is upon me, because he has anointed me to bring good news to the poor. He has sent me to proclaim release to the captives and recovery of sight to the blind, to let the oppressed go free, to proclaim the year of the Lord's favor. (Luke 4:18-19)

After Jesus said this, he went and did all these things. The Spirit came upon him when he was baptized, and he was called "Beloved Son" by his Father. He preached good news to the poor that the kingdom belonged to such people; he told of the great banquet that would be attended by the weak and financially humble. He proclaimed freedom for prisoners by releasing the demoniac and by taking Barrabas's place. He healed the blind beggar and many other sick people. He released the oppressed, the Gentiles, the Samaritans and many others that were hated and disregarded. He showed God's favor, as the widow at Nain proclaimed and as did many others who recognized Jesus' divinity. Jesus backed up his good news with good things. He was a blessing, but not in some ethereal, amorphic way. He blessed people in practical, understandable ways.

Jesus told the Good Samaritan story to articulate what it means for us to love our neighbors. Responding to a lawyer's attempt to define love in an immaterial way, Jesus tells a concrete story. It is painfully clear and practical. He tells us simply, "Go and do likewise." If we are to be good news, we can't bless people in mysterious, weird, religious ways that we alone understand. People need and want to see tangible things. Like the Good Samaritan, we all have means to bless people in real, practical, obvious ways. As people hear the good news from our lips, they should see the good news by our lives.

Greg and Jeff decided that they would be a presence of blessing in their dorm. They filled their room with everything the average college student needed: cold soft drinks, candy, Cup-O-Noodles, blue books and so on. They had a computer for all to use. Their room served the purposes of a school store, a library, a computer room and an entertainment center. They charged nothing and had a policy of always leaving their door open even if they were sleeping or away. They kept their room neat and took down offensive posters or religious paraphernalia so that all would feel welcomed and comfortable. Not surprisingly, their room was always full of people. When students were hungry in the middle of the night or when they needed someone to look over their essays, they went to Greg and Jeff's room.

Carrie, an elementary school teacher, found ample opportunity to bless her coworker Lisa. Lisa was a new teacher, and Carrie decided to aid her new friend. Carrie offered encouragement, helped Lisa set up her classroom, graded her papers and gave her ideas for art projects. Soon Lisa came to Carrie for other needs such as family concerns and friendship. They spent lunches together and got to know each other's families. Carrie prayed often that Lisa would be receiving the gospel as she tried to be good news in Lisa's life.

Telling Your Story

This is the easy part. Now that you have demonstrated what Christianity is like, it is easy to proclaim what Christianity is. For your friends you have crossed barriers with, stayed with and blessed in practical ways, your faith is no longer a set of abstract ideas. You don't have to be a person who understands the systemic underpinnings of the gospel—they have seen your life. Now tell your stories of Jesus.

The woman at the well, after an incredible conversation with Jesus, went and told her story. The demoniac, after being freed by Jesus, told his story to those who had known him in his harder days. The disciples, after being called by Jesus, called their friends by telling their stories. These people weren't arguing theology; they were telling stories that were hard to refute. Because they were known by these people, there wasn't room for theoretical discussion, only belief or unbelief.

In John 9 when Jesus healed the man born blind by putting some mud and spit in his face, many people wanted to argue theology. Who is this Jesus? Where did he get these powers from? Is he a heretic, or is he from God? The man's answer: "Well, you know I used to be blind. I am blind no more."

If you have lived faithfully with your friends, there will be room to tell your stories. They know you are a Christian. If you come back from a fellowship meeting and talk about what God did, it won't totally surprise them. When you come back from a church retreat and they ask how it was, don't shy away from saying God did some remarkable things. They might assume he did. Once you have these types of relationships, you can speak of Jesus to non-Christians in the same way you speak to Christians. You don't have to look for opportunities or manipulate conversations; simply let people know what God has done and is doing in your life. Use language that they can understand. If you are concerned that people might feel uncomfortable, then most likely they won't be; it is those who are not concerned about people's comfort who make them uncomfortable.

Once I went to a bachelor party with a bunch of friends. When the stripper came, with friends bantering, I went outside and sat on the curb. One of my friends followed me out and asked me what was wrong. With the sounds of music and cheering in the background, I told how Jesus had helped me deal with lust. He shared his own struggles.

After the blind man was grilled about who Jesus was, he told his story and simply asked those cross-examining him, "What do you believe? Is that man from God or is he not?" They had seen his life and heard his story. Now he was helping them make a decision for themselves.

When people hear our stories, they begin to see little chapters of the greater story of God. In the ways God is working in our lives, students will see grace and truth—a compelling mosaic of the gospel message. And they will be introduced to a larger story, the story of God who reached across time and space, across the incredible divide of sin to have a relationship with us.

What is evangelism? It's going and staying. It's blessing and telling. You have so much to offer others. Give it away and move your lips.

In what relationships should you be telling your story? Make it a point today to tell one of your coworkers or classmates about something Jesus has done in your life in the past week.

Living Your Faith

1. What groups or individuals is God calling you to spend more time with? Where do they hang out, what do they like to do and how can you be a part of it? What scares you about going?

2. Which relationships with non-Christians are difficult for you to stay in right now? What do you think Jesus is doing in that person's life? What do you need from Jesus to continue to be in that relationship?

3. Write a list of practical ways you can bless the non-Christians in your life. What are the resources you have—money, time, car, possessions, talents—that can be used to serve others practically?

4. In what relationships could you be telling your story? Today, tell one of your coworkers or classmates about something Jesus has done in your life this past week.

Recommended Reading

Jesus for a New Generation by Kevin Graham Ford, InterVarsity Press.

Even My Gold Press Card? video by Paul Tokunaga, TwentyOneHundred Productions (800-828-2100).

twenty-one

Knowing God's Heart
for the World
Amy Brooke

I WAS FIFTEEN, AND MY FAMILY WAS AT A BEACH ON THE EAST COAST. As one of my sisters and I rinsed off the floats in a tide pool one evening, a little girl and boy splashed by. The thought *Tell them not to play here* skirted across my mind. I dismissed it. It was their parents' job to keep an eye on them. *Tell them how deep it gets,* was the next thought. *Maybe I should say something.* Again, I reasoned that it wasn't my responsibility.

I dunked the raft once more and started to follow my family. "Amy!" I heard my name as clear as day from behind me (though no one I knew was back there). I turned to see the little boy going under and his sister fighting to keep her head above the water. I pulled the little girl out, and my sister pulled the little boy out from water where we could barely touch bottom.

I don't know if God called my name or what. Even though I didn't know their names or where they were from, I couldn't have lived with myself if I hadn't gotten involved. Looking back, I realize how close I came to missing a vital opportunity to be involved because I didn't think it was my responsibility.

God has a heart large enough for the world. As disciples our hearts should reflect his. However, on the whole, people—even God's people—rarely have time for anything that doesn't directly affect them. Sometimes we just don't have the time or the interest. Our pride and prejudices can get in the way. Sometimes we just don't care. We can be a lot like Jonah.

Jonah: The Reluctant Missionary

As a prophet of God, Jonah's job was to tell people the things God wanted them to know. When God told Jonah to go and warn the city of Nineveh about the coming judgment, he balked. Why should he go warn those dirty Assyrians? They worshiped a different god and had conquered his native Israel. *They didn't deserve a warning.* Jonah thought God's judging them would be a good idea. And if God needed any ideas about what to do to them, Jonah could give him a few.

After much convincing (including a submarine ride in the belly of a great fish), Jonah reluctantly did as God commanded. Just as Jonah feared, the Ninevites repented! They gave up their wicked ways and God suspended his judgment. Jonah was so angry at God's mercy, he wanted to die. Feeling used and misunderstood, Jonah wandered into the desert.

God decided it was time to teach Jonah a lesson. Seeing Jonah's discomfort in the intense sun, God made a vine miraculously grow to give Jonah shade. The next day God provided a worm to chew the vine so that it withered and died. This really got to Jonah.

> But God said to Jonah, "Do you have a right to be angry about the vine?"
> "I do," he said. "I am angry enough to die."
> But the LORD said, "You have been concerned about this vine, though you did not tend it or make it grow. It sprang up overnight and died overnight. But Nineveh has more than a hundred and twenty thousand people who cannot tell their right hand from their left, and many cattle as well. Should I not be concerned about that great city?" (Jonah 4:9-11 NIV)

Jonah was a man who cared little for those outside of Israel. He was grieved more by the death of a vine than by the possibility of 120,000 people dying. He knew little of God's heart.

In 1995 there was a massive earthquake in Kobe, Japan. I shuddered as I looked at the pictures of buildings collapsing, and I wondered if my father and his wife were okay. They lived there.

Living in the Midwest, I don't pay much attention to hurricane warnings. But in July 1996 Hurricane Greta threatened the coast of Florida. I paid attention. My sister, brother-in-law and young niece and nephew were threatened by Greta's fury.

Every time I turn on the news I hear stories about masses of people dying from wars, terrorist bombings, famines, earthquakes and floods. It has been that way all of my life. Yet unless someone I know is involved, the news rarely has an emotional impact on me. I'm more like Jonah than I would like to be.

What I *want* to be is less of a Jonah and more of a "world Christian"—someone who has a chunk of God's heart for all people in all places. A world Christian is not simply a missionary in a distant land. The Christian message is needed as much in the West as in the developing nations of the world. *Being a world Christian and a disciple is about developing a heart that increasingly resembles God's own heart.*

The starting point for such "heart surgery" is God's Word. One way I look at Scripture is to divide it into three simple sections: creation (Genesis 1-2), the fall (Genesis 3), and redemption (Genesis 4—Revelation). *Studying Scripture shows us that God's heart is about bringing a fallen world back into relationship with him.* His effort to do just that is what the majority of Scripture is about. Scripture is clear that God expects his people to join them in the effort.

A Promise and a Blessing

When God told Abram (later known as Abraham) to leave his home country and go to a distant land, he also made Abram a promise. "I will make of you a great nation, and I will bless you, and make your name great, *so that you will be a blessing.* I will bless those who bless you, and the one who curses you I will curse; and *in you all the families of the earth shall be blessed"* (Genesis 12:2-3, emphasis added).

This is an amazing promise: to make one person into a nation. That is what would have caught my attention if I had been Abram. Translated: "I'm going to be a really important person!" But God wasn't going to make Abram great for Abram's sake but for the sake of others. "So that you will be a blessing . . . in you all the families of the earth shall be blessed." God's intent was that Abram's offspring would be part of the plan for redeeming the world. Galatians 3:29 tells us that as Christians, we are Abraham's (Abram's) offspring.

Playing a part in redeeming the world was God's plan for the early church and is his plan for us today. Jesus' parting words to the disciples were, "Go therefore and make disciples of all nations, baptizing them in the name of the Father and of the Son and of the Holy Spirit, and teaching them to obey everything that I have commanded you. And remember, I am with you always, to the end of the age" (Matthew 28:19-20).

Becoming a World Christian

Before becoming more of a "world Christian" I needed to *acknowledge my responsibility to be involved.* Jesus tells a story in Matthew 25 about a man who had three servants. He gave the first servant ten talents, the second servant five and the third servant one. The first two servants used the money to make more money. The master was pleased. The third servant hid his talent. When the master asked for an accounting, he had nothing to show for it. Because the servant had not used the money to benefit his master, he was thrown outside. God holds us responsible for how we use our resources, money, time, skills and abilities.

Learning about missions and different cultures enables me to pray specifically. God answers general prayers, but by finding out more about a country it becomes possible to pray specifically. I was with a group that once prayed for Albania and thanked God that it was a predominantly Christian country. Unfortunately, that was far from true. According to *Operation World,* Albania is Europe's poorest country, with an unemployment rate of about 70 percent. It was once part of the Communist regime that tried to wipe out all religion. Currently 41.9 percent of the population has no religion, 40 percent is Muslim and *only 18 percent* of Albania is Christian. By knowing a little more about Albania, the prayers could have addressed real needs.

Good causes exceed my ability to invest myself and my resources in. *By learning and praying, I can let God direct my resources.* When a group asks for money and in learning about them I discover practices that seem to go against Scripture, I can discern that God would not want me using his resources to support such a cause. It is harder when there are several reputable causes to invest in. In that situation God allows us some freedom of choice and personality. We might also determine which needs seem greater.

Resources for Becoming a World Christian

☐ Get a copy of *Operation World* by Patrick Johnstone to find out how to pray specifically for various nations. It's updated regularly, so try the latest edition.

☐ Do an Internet search for information about different countries.

☐ Use the Internet to find a pen pal from another country.

☐ Write the embassy for the country you are interested in to obtain more information.

☐ Commit to keeping up on world news or at least the news in one or two countries.

☐ Get to know international students.

☐ Find out about missionaries your church supports. Think about corresponding with one of them.

☐ Consider attending InterVarsity's trienniel Urbana Mission Convention. Check out www.gospelcom.net/iv for more information.

Another example is when I decided to volunteer but didn't know what the real needs were. Through a local directory I found information about approximately thirty different groups who needed help. I went through the directory and marked the ones for which I was qualified, made a few calls and prayed. I finally decided on helping out at a local children's home. *I made the decision by doing a little investigating.*

While special cases come up at times, I tend to give to and pray regularly for only a handful of groups. This allows me to build relationships with the persons I support. As someone who raises financial support, I know how cared for and encouraged I've felt in having people stick with me over the long haul. They're also the ones who know the ins and outs of my ministry and how to pray most specifically for me.

Maybe the best reason for becoming a *world Christian* is the change it makes in us. After six weeks in Russia I was anxious to get home. I wanted to eat without wondering what I was eating, drink water without boiling it first, understand everything said to me, drive my car, use a feather pillow, not have to convert currency, use a washing machine and dryer, and so on. I didn't expect to miss much about Russia. A month after getting home I found myself gravitating to any newspaper or newscast with anything to say about Russia. My heart skipped for joy this morning to find an e-mail from a Russian I had gotten to know on my trip. Something changed during my time there. Either my heart got bigger or the world got smaller. Maybe it was a little of both. My heart looks a little more like God's.

Short-term Missions: Giving the World a Face
However, unless God completely rearranges my life, I doubt that I will ever be a long-term overseas missionary. That is okay. God uses different people in different ways. Having said that, *we should avail ourselves of opportunities to go short-term.* Numerous mission agencies have projects ranging from a week to a couple of months. A great way to find out about them is to attend InterVarsity Christian Fellowship's Urbana Missions Conference (see sidebar on facing page). Also local churches often sponsor shorter trips. Going with your church allows you to be a part of God's heart for the world, as well as to build relationships within your church.

Before I went to Russia, the faces I associated with Russia were those of Lenin, Stalin, Gorbachev, Yeltsin and whoever else happened to be in power and graced the six o'clock news. Now when I hear people talk about Russia, I think about Tatiana, my roommate on the trip who finally came to our last Bible study; Olga, a young but growing Christian; Elena, whose family worked from 7:00 a.m. to 2:00 p.m. to prepare a special meal for us and who cried as we left; Basil, who started reading the Bible he was given; and Alexa and others. Going short term helps us see why God cares so much for all the people of the world. *When you go short term, the world suddenly has a face.*

Another way to discover the face of the world is to *be involved in crossing cultures locally.* It can happen by choosing to attend a church that is predominately of a different race than you. It might mean helping out at a soup kitchen or another local mission agency. It can mean reaching out to Internationals at the local college or those working in your company. Wherever and however, it means getting to know someone from another culture on a personal level.

Long-term Missions: Changing the World's Face
Jesus told his disciples, "The harvest is plentiful, but the laborers are few; therefore ask the Lord of the harvest to send out laborers into his harvest" (Matthew 9:37-38). While we can be part of harvesting at home, it is important for each of us to ask, *"Is God asking me to do long-term missions overseas?"*

The statistics quoted in *The New Context of World Mission* are staggering to look at. They point to great need throughout the world. In the least evangelized parts of the world (countries like Bangladesh, parts of China and India, Pakistan, Turkey and Myanmar) there are over 1.1 billion people who probably won't hear the gospel unless someone goes to them. Five hundred people groups in this region have never heard the truth about Jesus, and of the approximately 332,000 missionaries in the world only 4,000 are deployed there.

If You Are Thinking About Going Overseas Long Term . . .
□ **Know Scripture.** Find someone to help you learn to really dig into God's Word.
□ **Get involved in a local fellowship.** You will need and want a church family that supports you with their prayers, encouragement and money.
□ **Find out what life "on the field" is like.** Talk to missionaries when you have the opportunity.
□ **Read missionary biographies and autobiographies.**
□ **House a crosscultural missionary on furlough.**
□ **Research mission agencies.** (An Urbana Missions Conference is a fabulous place to be introduced to hundreds of excellent agencies.)
□ **Find a mentor.** Talk to your pastor. Let people know what you are thinking so they can help guide you.
□ **Pray about your future.**
□ **Pray for current missionaries.**
□ **Keep up on the news from the area of the world you are interested in.**

☐ Find out what schooling, skills or language you might need.

☐ Get your feet wet by going short term.

☐ Consider working in a secular business office overseas (also called tent-making) and sharing the gospel. Business people are admitted to countries where missionary visas are limited or impossible to come by.

Is God whispering (or shouting) in your ear to be involved? Do you think that it isn't your responsibility, that someone else will take care of the praying, giving or going? Think again! Ask yourself, *Does my heart resemble Jonah's or God's?* Take some steps today to make it resemble God's heart. A disciple's heart must reflect God's heart.

Living Your Faith

1. Describe how God's heart and Jonah's differed. Is your heart more like Jonah's or God's? Why?

2. What evidence in Scripture is there of God's concern for the entire world?

3. Name three major world events in the last week. If you can't, go to the library and look at international newspapers. How do you think God feels about those events? How do you feel?

4. What steps can you take today to become a *world Christian*?

Recommended Reading:

Your Mission, Should You Accept It by Stephen Gaukroger, InterVarsity Press.

Shadow of the Almighty by Elisabeth Elliott, HarperSanFrancisco.

Six Dangerous Questions to Transform Your View of the World by Paul Borthwick, InterVarsity Press.

twenty-two

Following Jesus
in the Dark
Robbie Castleman

EDNA, MY FRIEND, HAD BEEN MURDERED. BRUTALLY. SHE HAD been beaten, strangled and then set on fire in her own home.

Breck, my husband, told me this when I returned home from an errand. I was still sitting in my car. When he told me, as gently as he could, I remember pounding my fists into the steering wheel and sobbing, "Jesus, where were you?"

And there was no reply.

Edna's sweetheart, Charlie, came to live with us for a while, to be with us in his grief. A few months before, Charlie and Edna had joined the church my husband pastored. Breck had baptized Charlie, who had been a broken and abandoned drug abuser for many years. After a week, and a trip to take roses to Edna's grave, Charlie returned to his own place.

Three days later we found out why Charlie's phone kept ringing unanswered, why he didn't come to the door when we knocked. The police called to tell us that Charlie was dead, and they needed someone to identify the body. At first it seemed likely that death came from his own hand, and this added to our anguish. But then we learned that it was Charlie's heart that killed him. His heart, made older over the years by drugs and now broken by grief, had suffered a massive heart attack.

I hurt very badly. I ached with the heaviness of those days and weeks. I asked God many questions and received no answers. I begged God for comfort, and he was silent. I took no joy in the victories of faith experienced by others.

However, in the incredible sense of abandonment during that time, in all that pain, I began to understand that discipleship includes profound suffering. I've never felt so distant from God than when I have felt so close to the suffering of Jesus. In God's silence I began to hear his heartbeat.

Being a disciple is following Jesus into the experiences of his life. Jesus suffered. And the Scriptures tell us over and over again that sharing the suffering of our Savior is connected with sharing in his glory.

"We suffer with him so that we may also be glorified with him.

"I consider that the sufferings of this present time are not worth comparing with the glory about to be revealed to us." (Romans 8:17-18)

"I want to know Christ and the power of his resurrection and the sharing of his sufferings by becoming like him in his death, if somehow I may attain the resurrection from the dead." (Philippians 3:10-11)

"But rejoice insofar as you are sharing Christ's sufferings, so that you may also be glad and shout for joy when his glory is revealed." (1 Peter 4:13)

Disciples Risk Suffering

Following Jesus will mean knowing what he has known, feeling what he has felt. And the Scriptures make it very clear that God, in Christ, suffers. Jesus knew pain. Jesus knew what it was like to be abandoned. Jesus knew the incredible anguish of crying out and hearing nothing but empty silence. "My God, my God, why have you forsaken me?" Following Jesus, being his disciples, may bring us to times in our lives when the only prayer we can pray is this prayer—the prayer he also uttered.

In the aftermath of Edna's and Charlie's deaths, suffering and dying with Christ was no longer just good Pauline theology. It was painful. It was excruciating. It all hurt so badly because I had loved Charlie and Edna. I had taken risks in getting close to their sometimes-turbulent lives. I had been a midwife at their rebirths, nurtured their faith and taught them how to walk in Christ.

It's risky to be committed to closeness in this age of apartness. It's risky to really know people. Jesus took the risk of really loving and knowing and living with people—messy people. Discipleship is being known by Jesus. And it is knowing Jesus so well that we do what he would do, hear with his heart, feel his concerns and join him in his work in the world. It's loving others with his heart and risking heartbreak.

Discipleship is following Jesus, putting ourselves in his place and experiencing what he has. Often our biggest problem with discipleship is our unwillingness to take a risk that might result in suffering. We don't allow ourselves to be in the unsafe, untamed places where we can experience what he did. Jesus suffered.

We avoid pain, pressure, discomfort. But Jesus didn't. He didn't play it safe. He went over the top, out on the edge, and he suffered for it. He let himself love people who would betray him. He healed lepers he knew would not return to give thanks. While we were his enemies, he died for us! Disciples risk loving like he did, being rejected like he was and are willing to die in the agony of abandonment.

Disciples have hearts that break over the things that break God's heart, over people who will not listen, over the lost who will not be found, over the world of sin that kills Edna, destroys Charlie and wounds those who are precious to us. Disciples weep over Jerusalem and suffer in holy silence from the blows of people who don't know who we really are.

Disciples feed the hungry not just from the overflow of their cupboards but off their plates. Disciples give a cup of cold water to the thirsty and risk experiencing their own thirst. Disciples take risks for the gospel and lose their lives for dying people.

Mature disciples have learned that following Jesus isn't limited to a good quiet time, a weekly Bible study, regular worship and healthy relationships. Mature disciples follow Jesus when quiet times are dry, the Word makes no sense, worship is stale and relationships are hard. When God withholds the very things we need, disciples follow Jesus because all they want is him.

Satisfied with Nothing

Psalm 131, someone said, is a very short one to read, but a very long one to learn. The second verse reads like this

> Surely I have composed and quieted my soul;
> Like a weaned child rests against his mother,
> My soul is like the weaned child within me. (NASB)

"Like a weaned child with its mother." What is a "weaned" child? It's a child that is no longer a nursing infant. A weaned child does not rest in his mother's arms to be fed, filled and satisfied. A weaned child "with its mother" desires nothing of her but to be with her. Charles Spurgeon commented on this psalm once. He wrote:

> The transition from a suckling infant to a weaned child, from a squalling baby to a quiet son or daughter is not smooth. It is stormy and noisy. It is no easy thing to quiet yourself . . . it is a pitched battle. The baby is denied expected comforts and flies into rage and sinks into sulks. There are sobs and struggles. The infant is facing its first great sorrow and it is in sore distress. But, to the weaned child his mother is his comfort though she has denied him comfort. It is a blessed mark of growth out of spiritual infancy when we can forgo the joys which once appeared to be essential, and can find our solace in Him who denies them to us. *(The Treasury of David)*

Disciples Risk Dying

Disciples don't explain away real suffering; they enter into it. They learn to trust the Lord they have known in the light when all around is darkness. I learned this during an experience I shared with a dear friend, and through a Scripture study in the book of Job.

Pam telephoned me on a Sunday morning in September. A small plane carrying her husband of two years and four other mission workers had crashed into the frigid Gulf of Alaska. A search had just been started, and Pam wanted me to pray and to ask other friends across the lower forty-eight states to pray as well. We did. Fervent prayers of love and faith were lifted around the clock. The plane was never found.

Why? Why couldn't the Creator have stilled the storm? Refueled tanks?

Intervened in some way? In Scripture Daniel's three friends walked out of a fiery furnace without even the smell of smoke! Why not now? Why not always?

Journal/Sept. 27: My five-year-old son voiced the question the day before yesterday. Aware that Bill was killed in a plane crash, he seemed understandably anxious that "Mama" was flying in a plane to Alaska. Trying to reassure him, I said, "Well, Scottie, Mama will be safe in the plane. Jesus will be with Mama." After a pause, Scott simply responded, "But, Mama, Jesus was with Mr. Bill, too."

Although I wanted to sit in pseudosecurity, my son would not let me stay there. I wanted to sit in the sure comfort of Job's friends when they came to see him in his suffering. Job tried to call his friends into reality, but they answered him with logic and cold reason. His comforters concluded that Job suffered because he or his ancestors had sinned. "You reap what you sow" was their unspoken slogan. Job's friends were eager to explain his suffering, not because they were intentionally callous but to escape from their own vulnerability. If Job really were a righteous person, how precarious would their own reap-what-you-sow security become. God's sovereignty had to remain predictable, manageable.

Although awestruck by the mechanics, God was still a "vending machine" deity to all but Job. You insert righteous works, pull the knob of prayer and out comes prosperity, descendants, security. Insert sin and out comes suffering and loss. Job's friends Eliphaz, Bildad and Zophar first implied and then declared that Job was getting what he deserved.

I wanted to reassure my son by presenting him with a predictable God who was easy to explain. I knew the assurance I gave Scott was not honest. I had to face the reality of a God who was not predictable and seemingly unjust.

Journal/Oct. 18: Pam and I talked a lot about the danger of coldness and cynicism creeping into our relationship with God because of being "thrown a curve." Pam said, "It's hard right now to expect anything good from God." True. It all makes me a little "gun shy." I do know that faith should not, cannot be centered around what God *does,* but who God *is.* It's hard to pare down to essentials this core of faith.

God's will cannot be reduced to a predictable pattern of anthropomorphic benevolence—goodness defined by what makes people happy. God's hand is not manipulated by the grandest works of righteous people, neither by the most meaningful rituals nor the most fervent prayers of love and faith. Job's friends are the patron saints of Christianity in the modern West, which panders guaranteed health and prosperity for the cost of a thirty-minute quiet time, reliable tithing and a fish symbol on our rear bumper.

Vending-machine believers look through Eliphaz's eyes and see suffering as the exclusive property of the foolish. They close their eyes with Bildad and do not admit to a world where the wicked often do prosper and evil breeds success. Standing with Zophar are Christians who pigeonhole the options of the Almighty into simplistic formulas to "stand on" and "claim."

Journal/Sept. 21: Help me, Lord, to comfort Pam with a reminder of your presence, the one thing now that we do know for certain. Keep us from seeking comfort in the explanation of the circumstances, things we cannot know for certain.

It is a fragile faith that is sustained by answers. Job's friends had a faulty faith because they thought they had the answers. Job stumbled because he demanded an answer and felt he was due one. Acts 12 is known as the miraculous-deliverance-of-Peter chapter, not the martyrdom-of-James chapter. In verse 2 James is dead; in verse 7 Peter is delivered from jail—in fact, verse 8 says the angel even makes sure Peter doesn't forget his coat or his shoes! James loses his head, and Peter gets to keep his sandals. How do we trust God, whom we know is "the same yesterday, today and forever" in the face of such unpredictability?

Journal/Sept.30: In my struggle to comfort Pam, I have considered the fact that suffering can appear to be without purpose or good benefit from our perspective. "All things" don't always look like they "work together for good." My faith, as Pam's, must not root itself in the good we can see, but in the absolute, immutable goodness of God we do not see. God is good. Always. This we must believe by faith, not by sight.

The realities of life declare that God's people are not immune to suffering. There are also realities beyond our perception or understanding. Job never knew that it was his righteousness that fit him for the "contest" he entered and won. He never knew the first chapter of the book that bears his name, but he insisted page after page that God alone could be his vindicator. Job had nowhere else to go. He surrendered to the singular necessity of trusting God no matter what.

> *Journal/Sept. 18:* The search for the plane has stopped. The death of these missionaries, I think, is a mighty steep price for God to get something done. The radio station may now secure its funding. Someone has come to know Jesus. Oh, but could not God's Spirit have done his will at less cost? There is little comfort even in the most desirable side-effects. But, it did cost God his only Son to buy me back. There was purpose only he could see. Where was God's comfort?

The comfort I shared with Pam was often silent. I quietly packed the boxes of clothes and books she could not pack. I wrote the letters she could not write. I listened when she needed to remember. And I prayed for her when she could not pray, when it all hurt so very badly. And with timidity I helped point to a hope that Pam could not see clearly through her tears. I reminded her of a glory to come through the suffering she shared with her Savior.

God may not have intervened, may not have stepped in to undo what broke our hearts. The plane went down. Bill died. We may not understand why God intervened for Peter and not for James. Why some and not all? Why then and not now? All that disciples know is a point in history that gives us hope in tragedy, a point of divine intervention that spans all time: God raised Jesus from the dead.

The tomb is still empty. And this alone should be the focus, the singular zenith of our hope, the only resource for unfailing joy. The fact of the resurrection, our only honest comfort, is the foundation of a faith that trusts God, no matter what.

> *Journal/Jan. 3:* Well, it's a new year. I've been thinking about Pam and my study in Job. Before Satan came, God knew the results of the contest because he knew the heart of his servant Job. God knows the heart of his servant Pam, today. God sees the victory of faith in her life. I don't desire such a contest for myself, but I do desire that God would work in my heart such faith so that he could ask, "Have you considered my servant Robbie?" and know the contest won!

Following Jesus leads to suffering. It is true that we cannot see God face-to-face and live. This does not mean that no one has seen God. It means that when we do, we die. And that is a painful and wonderful thing.

It is painful because it costs us—not a little but everything. We will suffer and die. And it is wonderful because, like the Savior, we live again. We will awake in the arms of our heavenly Parent, and there we will rest and be content. Disciples compose and quiet their souls. A disciple rests like a weaned child with unanswered questions, with pain and want—we rest in the shadow of the Lord we follow and know what it is to suffer and be loved.

There is no formula for dying in Christ. It is not fun, not even satisfying in itself. It hurts. It is not easy. We do not seek it, but we do risk it. This is the way of the disciple and the only way to glory. In times of suffering God has not dried my tears. He has reminded me that he has shed them too. And when my tears mingle with his, when my heart breaks over the wages of sin, when I risk loving the "least of these" like he did, I have been his disciple.

Living Your Faith

1. Identify a time and circumstance in your life where you felt like the Lord was absent. What helped you through that time?

2. Think about someone who might be in a difficult, sad or lonely situation. Pray for him or her. How might you help this person through this time?

3. Who are the challenging, difficult and "messy" people in your community or church? What can you do to risk ministry to them? What support would you need to make this investment?

4. Read the book of Job with a friend and talk about it in the light of how people see suffering and faith today both inside and outside the church.

Recommended Reading

Suffering (Lifeguide Bible Study) by Jack Kuhatschek, InterVarsity Press.
When God Interrupts by Craig Barnes, InterVarsity Press.

twenty-three

Hope When You Fall
Amy Brooke

HE DIED ON JANUARY 21, 1924, BUT OVER SEVEN DECADES LATER I stood in line to view his body in a guarded mausoleum in Moscow's Red Square. Vladimir Ilyich Lenin helped usher Communism into Russia, and for some he was a savior, the ultimate source of hope for a better future. But Communism is no longer the leading force in Russia. As I viewed Lenin's body in 1998, I wondered, *What good is a hope that is dead?*

A friend once asked, "Do you have hope?" I had to think for a minute. Sometimes I don't *feel* very hopeful. Some of the sins I struggled with ten years ago, I struggle with today. Some of the things that gave me pain years ago still bring tears to my eyes. I still fail miserably, sometimes on a daily basis. But I do have hope. *Having hope is some of the essence of what it means to follow Jesus.* I am not the same person I was yesterday or the day before. I have hope for some of the same reasons that Peter did.

Peter Blew It

His given name was Simon, but Jesus nicknamed him Peter. He was hot-headed, impetuous and an enthusiastic follower of Jesus. When Peter got things right, he nailed them. Take the day Jesus asked his disciples who the people said that he was. The crowds thought that he was John the Baptist or the ancient prophet Elijah come back from the dead. Then Jesus made it more personal. "Who do you say I am?" Peter answered without hesitation, "You are the Christ." Peter got the most vital question right.

But Peter wasn't perfect. When Jesus began to teach his disciples that he would have to suffer and die, Peter rebuked the one he had confessed as the Christ, the holy one of God. Jesus was angry. "But turning and looking at his disciples, he rebuked Peter and said, 'Get behind me, Satan! For you are setting your mind not on divine things but on human things'" (Mark 8:33).

But the failure that must have plagued Peter the most came the night before Jesus died. Jesus predicted that all of the disciples would desert him, but Peter was insistent that he wouldn't. "Jesus said to him, 'Truly I tell you, this day, this very night, before the cock crows twice, you will deny me three times'" (Mark 14:30). He still insisted he would die before disowning Jesus.

Then it happened. Jesus was arrested and taken to trial. As Peter waited outside, three people accused him of being one of Jesus' followers. Three times, out of fear, he denied knowing Jesus. The cock crowed. Peter wept. In spite of his best intentions, he failed.

If Jesus knew how badly Peter would fail, why did he call him in the first place?

As a perfectionist I perpetually feel like a failure in my Christian life. Why can't I ever be completely consistent in my Scripture study? Why is prayer so hard for me? Why can't I be kinder and nicer and gentler? I really try, so why do my efforts seem to amount to so little?

I went on a mission trip to Russia for six weeks. At the end of the second week a man on a bus inappropriately touched me, and I witnessed a confrontation between one of our leaders and a drunk man with a knife. No one was physically hurt in either situation, but all sense of safety fled me.

Like Peter, I began to make self-centered decisions. Concerns about safety overrode anything I thought God might want me to do. Like Peter, I wept over my failure. When I fail, I want to hide from God.

Peter responded differently. After a night of fishing the disciples saw

Jesus on the beach. Rather than cowering in the boat, Peter jumped into the
water and swam to shore. What allowed Peter to so enthusiastically greet
the God he failed? *Hope.*

Hope That Won't Fail

Hope, by the world's standards, is unpredictable. Hope, by biblical standards, is an unchangeable promise rooted in an unchanging God of grace.

Peter's hope in God's love allowed him to jubilantly greet Jesus. Jesus
knew Peter would deny him. If Jesus had intended to abandon Peter to his
own devices, he surely would have done it before Peter had a chance to fail
him. Luke 22 records that Jesus even prayed for Peter's later restoration.
Peter's freedom came in the depth of the knowledge of Jesus' love. In
Knowing God J. I. Packer writes, "There is tremendous relief in knowing
that His love to me is utterly realistic, based at every point on a prior
knowledge of the worst about me, so that no discovery now can disillusion
him about me, in the way that I am so often disillusioned about myself, and
quench His determination to bless me."

God is full of truth. He will never deny our failures. But he is also a God
of grace who holds us fast in the midst of those failures and invites us to
further ministry. That morning, Jesus fed Peter breakfast and then, knowing
Peter's sense of failure, pulled him away for a private talk.

When they had finished breakfast, Jesus said to Simon Peter, "Simon son of John,
do you love me more than these?" He said to him, "Yes, Lord; you know that I love
you." Jesus said to him, "Feed my lambs." A second time he said to him, "Simon
son of John, do you love me?" He said to him, "Yes, Lord; you know that I love
you." Jesus said to him, "Tend my sheep." He said to him the third time, "Simon
son of John, do you love me?" Peter felt hurt because he said to him the third time,
"Do you love me?" And he said to him, "Lord, you know everything; you know
that I love you." Jesus said to him, "Feed my sheep. Very truly, I tell you, when you
were younger, you used to fasten your own belt and to go wherever you wished. But
when you grow old, you will stretch out your hands, and someone else will fasten a
belt around you and take you where you do not wish to go." (He said this to indicate the kind of death by which he would glorify God.) After this he said to him,
"Follow me." (John 21:15-19)

Jesus asked Peter three times—seemingly, once for each denial—if Peter loved him. Each time Peter responded with an affirmation. Each time Jesus told Peter to take care of Jesus' sheep. Peter needed to know that failure had not cut him off from service and relationship with Jesus.

The same love that held fast when Peter failed holds fast when we fail. We need never be afraid to take our failures to God.

Peter had hope because he knew a risen Savior. Peter had seen Jesus' body wrapped and placed in a tomb. Three days later, a handful of women had come to finish preparing the body for the grave. When they arrived, the tomb was empty and a risen Jesus appeared to them. Jesus conquered death, an unalterable of life. This fact compelled Peter toward Jesus. *No other religion has the testimony of a living Savior who has faced death and won.*

Our hope rests in the fact that the same power that was at work in raising Jesus from the dead is at work in those who love God. "I pray also that the eyes of your heart may be enlightened in order that you may know the hope to which he has called you, the riches of his glorious inheritance in the saints, and his incomparably great power for us who believe. That power is like the working of his mighty strength, which he exerted in Christ when he raised him from the dead and seated him at his right hand in the heavenly realms." (Ephesians 1:18-20 NIV). That same power is changing us into the people God wants us to be.

Realities of the Race

We sometimes hear stories of miraculous changes. On the night a drug user becomes a Christian, all desire or need for drugs disappears. Or someone with a violent temper suddenly becomes very gentle and never again raises his hand to another. God's power can change people instantly, but for most of us it is a longer process.

Recently I was chatting with a woman I know from work. We discovered that at times we both struggle with depression, self-esteem issues and knowing how much God loves us. "I thought I had this under control," she said. "I keep coming back to it." We both want to know why it seems to be taking so long.

Perhaps *not* having the struggles in our lives "zapped" is a special blessing. As painful as running the race and falling can be, there is a comfort in being picked up and encouraged along the way. It is in the process of the race that we learn the most about ourselves and God's love and mercy for us.

But I get discouraged with the race. Each time I return to an "old" issue, I feel like I've gone backward. Rather than running on a straight road, perhaps we race up a curving mountain path. I should not be surprised to see the same landscape, the same boulder or tree, time and again. I need to recognize, however, that I've gone higher and have a different view. Each time I struggle with it, God has something new to show me about the struggle or myself or himself. Growth is more often cyclical rather than linear.

I have a tendency toward clinical depression; it's something that lasts months and is often biochemical. Depression isn't a sin, but some of the ways I cope are. I become hard to reason with, grow angry and cut myself off from friends and God. Times with God cease to exist and everything becomes someone else's responsibility.

As frustrating as each depressive episode may be, I have grown. The first time it happened, I didn't know what was going on and I simply reacted. I recognized the symptoms more quickly the second time. I got help even more quickly the next time. I've learned how to manage some of the symptoms. I force myself to stay connected to people and, most importantly, to God. It still feels lousy, but I handle the situation better each time because of what I learned the last time around. I'm "racing" up a mountain and growing.

Peter didn't like it when Jesus said that he (Christ) would have to suffer and die and three days later rise again. Peter must have gained tremendous hope when those words were fulfilled. If the most incredulous prediction—rising from the dead—came true, it surely validated everything else Jesus had promised his followers: that he would be with them to the end of the age, that he was going to prepare a place for them, that he would never leave them or forsake them and that they would see his glory.

That day on the beach, Jesus gave Peter a personal prophecy. Peter had insisted he would die for Jesus and had failed. Jesus acknowledged that this failure wasn't the end of the story. He told Peter that he would glorify God with his death; in the end he would not deny his Lord. What wasn't possible at one point became possible as Peter continued his mountain race.

I'm an identical twin. While being a twin has perks, the biggest pitfall is comparison. One of my most difficult childhood experiences was being in a lower reading group than my sister for two years. I asked myself why I wasn't as smart as she was. That experience wrongly convinced me that I was less intelligent than my sister. There will always be someone smarter, taller, stronger, more beautiful and more spiritual. Comparison is always a detriment to hope because it takes our eyes off of our living hope.

Peter wasn't immune. His response to Jesus' statement was "What about that guy over there? Am I going to do better than him?" Jesus said, "Don't worry about him. Just be concerned about you. *You*, follow me." Our eyes need to look forward to God and nowhere else.

Follow me. Two key words. They were among the first Jesus ever said to Peter. And they were among the last. *Follow me.* Those words are at the core of what it means to have faith on the edge, to follow Jesus.

Looking Heavenward: A Short Bible Study

1. Read Revelation 7:9-17. How is the multitude described?
2. What is the multitude's response to being in the presence of the Lamb of God? What do you think your response would be?
3. What do you think the great ordeal in verse 14 is? Imagine what it would be like.
4. How do you think the great ordeal compares to the benefits the multitude now has?
5. Looking over these verses, what do you think the chief goal of the Christian is? How might the way we live our lives accomplish this?

We also have hope because God doesn't believe in cliffhangers. While we don't know all of the twists and turns the plots of our lives may take, we do know the end of the story. Even though we toil on earth, heaven is the destiny of all who follow Jesus, that is, those who have washed their robes white in the blood of the Lamb.

Picture it. You are among a great multitude. On your right a Japanese man hooks arms with a Korean man as they sing God's praises. On your left a woman from Guatemala bows low in worship. Farther ahead, a black South African man dances praise to God with a little blond girl high on his shoulders. All focus is on the Lamb on the throne. You know peace like you have never known. You're utterly safe. You are home, never to be hungry or thirsty or tired or scared or lonely again. God has personally wiped all your tears away. You can't help but shout praises to God, your living and unchangeable hope.

Hope and endurance for the race come from staying focused on a God who fully knows us yet fully loves us, who has risen from the dead, who keeps his promises and who will one day welcome us home. Our sole responsibility is to keep running the race no matter how long it takes or how often we fall. As the author of Hebrews writes:

> Therefore, since we are surrounded by such a great cloud of witnesses, let us throw off everything that hinders and the sin that so easily entangles, and let us run with perseverance the race marked out for us. Let us fix our eyes on Jesus, the author and perfecter of our faith, who for the joy set before him endured the cross, scorning its shame, and sat down at the right hand of the throne of God. Consider him who endured such opposition from sinful men, so that you will not grow weary and lose heart. (Hebrews 12:1-3 NIV)

Whatever your situation, your hope is sure. Stake your life on it!

Living Your Faith

1. How do you handle failure in life? In your Christian walk?

2. Think about your biggest failure. What reasons do you have to hope about that situation?

3. How might knowing the end of the story that God has promised help you deal with difficulties now?

4. How have you experienced God's love and mercy in the midst of failure?

5. What does it mean to "fix your eyes on Jesus?" Brainstorm some practical ways you might be able to do that.

Recommended Reading

Invitation to a Journey by Robert Mulholland Jr., InterVarsity Press.

Hope Has Its Reasons by Rebecca Manley Pippert, InterVarsity Press (forthcoming, fall 2000).

twenty-four

Keeping the Faith
Paul Tokunaga

I LIKE TO COOK. WHY? I LOVE TO EAT. I ESPECIALLY LIKE VEGETA-bles. One of the most intriguing things I've encountered is the arti-choke. Most people today think artichokes are those army-green chunks sitting in pickled water in little jars. Eating artichokes—the whole artichoke—is a lost art form today.

Artichokes grow on thick bushes that can grow four to five feet high. I grew up with several in our backyard. (One of our truly hilarious family jokes was "You oughta choke . . . on an awta-choke! Har, har, har!")

The edible part is the flower head, from a small to large fist in size. The flower head is composed of layers of leaves that become meatier and more tender as you get to the heart of the artichoke.

Most people boil their artichokes; little cloves of garlic inserted between the leaves enhance the flavor quite nicely. The leaves are peeled off one by one, dipped in a hollandaise sauce (drawn butter is not a bad second choice), and then you sort of gnaw off the meaty part with your lower front teeth. Don't eat this with someone around whom you're trying to be suave.

Now if that doesn't make your mouth water and send you running to the grocery store, this will. After you've gnawed about twenty to thirty leaves, you'll notice the texture dramatically changes. The leaves get very soft. You *carefully* pull those apart. You then encounter another layer of very fine leaves with thistly tips. *Very fine.* You must discipline yourself not to rip it apart, because if you do, you ruin the *piece résistance* of the artichoke: its heart.

The heart of the artichoke (I'm not describing those things choking in pickle juice) is exquisite. It's usually the size of those dollar pancakes at IHOP, stacked three high. It's not much to look at, but you didn't get this far simply to stare at it.

You'll have saved some of the sauce for the heart. With your fingers break off a piece and dip. A deep breath helps here. Place it on the tip and then the middle of your tongue, letting it sit; then swirl a bit before you slowly chew. Whatever you do, don't be a wild animal and swallow the chunk whole. You will have missed the whole point.

A Slow God in a Fast World

We live in an antiwhole-artichoke culture. Ours is an artichoke-*heart* culture. We don't want to mess with the leaves: too slow, too tedious, not enough payoff for the work involved. *Just gimme dat heart.* In other words, we want the best now. We want results now—no time to go slowly and savor life's best offerings.

Look at us: our pagers tell us to use our cell phones so we can make the call back *immediately.* We don't sit and wait in the drive-through lane at the bank if the line is longer than four or five cars. Our laptops are never quite fast enough. We *need,* we *must have,* those extra bps's, gigabytes and megahertzes so we can conquer any project, e-mail any-one—anywhere, at anytime—and fax that information before they can even get to their machine.

Such frenetic activity spills over into our life with God and our expectations of him. We pray, tap our toes five times (we call it "waiting on God"), then lurch forward with what we hope is a word from him. More likely it's just the afterburn of the burrito we had for lunch. Truth is, *we follow a slow*

God in a fast world. Not that God is really slow. It's just that we are cali-
brated to such high speeds, anything or anyone that doesn't maintain our
pace seems to just plod along.

Terry Morrison, a veteran campus minister, once said in a talk, "Slow
down. Do less. Do better."

You've just about finished reading a book that has tried to cover a lot of
ground. With each chapter you may be thinking, *oh great, here's one more
thing I need to do to be a growing Christian.* And like IOUs stacked high
on a pile, following Jesus starts feeling overwhelming—a load too heavy to
bear.

Lest you consider bailing, here are a few suggestions to help this book
continue working for you and within you in the days and years ahead.

Faith on a Few Edges

First, once you've finished chapter twenty-four of *Faith on the Edge,* don't
push yourself to grow in your faith on *every* edge. One or two or three for
now—not twenty-four—will do just fine. Rome wasn't built in a day;
maturity in Christ doesn't happen in four years of college or even in your
first five years out of school. You've got the rest of your life to look increasingly more like Jesus.

Let God speak to you—through his Word and Spirit, through Christian
friends and through your family—about a couple of areas in which you
should sink your roots deeply for a while. It may be in the area of evangelism or serving the poor or racial reconciliation or developing deeper relationships with your parents or taking the "healing journey" toward personal
wholeness. Who knows? *Faith on the Edge* was designed to cover the
"waterfront" of discipleship for college-aged to young adults in the early
twenty-first century. Now let God speak to you about "Faith on the Edge:
The Saga Continues." In other words, let him show you what risky faith
will look like for you. Who knows? God knows.

If you have a mentor or discipler in your life, discuss the "what next"
and "how" questions with him or her. This person knows you and wants the
best for you. Trust your mentor for some good advice. If you don't have
someone like that, talk it over with another maturing Christian.

Think Long, Think Thirty-five

When I was a kid, a bunch of us were always playing football in the street. The play of choice for quarterback-of-the-day was simple, Go long. The rest of his team would sprint with arms flailing and legs pumping, and he'd heave the ball as far as he could. Occasionally ball and receiver were in harmony, and we had street-football bliss.

So second, go long, or rather *think* long. Think of your life long-term— when you're really old, say, thirty-five. Don't give up your goals and dreams; just stretch out the timeline. Thinking long-term gives you a better shot at achieving them. What qualities do you want to dominate your life at thirty-five? (If you're already past thirty-five, add fifteen or twenty years.) What values will transform you? What character traits do you want to define your life? What do you want your legacy to be at age thirty-five? Don't be shy—aim high!

Benjamin Mays, former president of Morehouse College, put it well: "It must be borne in mind that the tragedy of life doesn't lie in not reaching your goal. The tragedy lies in having no goal to reach. It isn't a calamity to die with dreams unfulfilled, but it is a calamity not to dream. It is not a disgrace not to reach the stars, but it is a disgrace to have no stars to reach for. Not failure, but low aim is sin."

What do you want your life characterized by when you are thirty-five?

Give Yourself Grace

Third, give yourself grace when you fall. You can because God already has. God in Christ reeks of grace. Woe to us if he didn't. As I study Scripture, I watch God bend over backwards "by any means necessary" to win people over to his side. Ultimately, "by any means necessary" led him to allow his son, Jesus, to die on a cross in order to win our allegiance and loyalty. Given our propensity toward broken promises and messing up, that's a lot of grace.

In the Scriptures we find a God who is a combination of justice and mercy: tough when he has to be and forgiving people when we don't deserve it. This God of second and third chances gives Peter "the betrayer" the chance to become Peter "the rock." God invests himself in a cold-hearted killer like Saul so he could later become the tender lover Paul. And we see a God willing to leave the ninety-nine sheep in the flock to find the one who had strayed, and God is ecstatic when he finds it. He is a God who weeps with those who are devastated by anguish and pain.

God in Christ reeks of grace for you and me. But here's the kicker: "A person has to get fed up with the ways of the world before he, before she, acquires an appetite for the world of grace" (Eugene Peterson, *A Long Obedience in the Same Direction*). Are you fed up? If you have failed miserably, chin up. Admit your failure and throw yourself back onto the lap of the One who is waiting to catch and to carry you on his shoulders back home.

Give Yourself Away to Others

Fourth, as a growing follower of Jesus it is also important that you give your life away to others. Whom might you *disciple?* Don't let that word scare you away. In your fellowship or church is there a friend younger in the faith who would benefit from spending regular time with you? If this book has helped you grow, consider taking a younger believer through it. Some of my greatest times of growth have come through discipling a younger Christian; God has used our times together to point out areas of growth needed in my own life.

Roger: God's Straight Line

C. S. Lewis eloquently summed up the Christian life: "The good news of the Gospel is that God draws straight lines with crooked sticks."

Roger was one of those crooked sticks. He was born with a serious defect. The doctors told his mom and dad he wouldn't live. He miraculously survived birth, but one set of vocal chords was paralyzed. The doctors said he'd never talk. He learned to talk. Roger grew up with an extremely scratchy, deep voice. He was hard to understand at times, but he could speak.

His dad died when he was young. Roger came to Christ right before he went to Florida State University as a freshman. He immediately got involved in the InterVarsity group. As the FSU staff worker I asked Roger if he'd like me to disciple him. "Yes!" was his immediate reply. He was so eager to grow.

My first impression of Roger, truthfully, was that he was not a winner. Along with his weak voice, he was kind of scrawny. He was also a straight shooter. You knew what he thought, but he could be pretty blunt, sometimes abrasive. One thing I noticed right away about Roger as we began to meet, he had deep joy. "Roger, how can you be so joyful—nearly dying, losing your dad, the problems with your voice?" I queried. Roger answered, "Paul, when you almost die at birth, you are just overwhelmed to be alive."

His freshman year was drawing to a close. During one of our last weekly get-togethers, he told me, "God is calling me into church-planting in another country. I'm leaving FSU. I'm transferring to Bible college." Normally any campus worker would do flips over a student making a commitment to missions, as a freshman no less. But something wasn't clicking, so I prayed and chewed on it the following week.

We met in The Streak, the campus snack bar. I told Roger, "Somehow, it doesn't seem right to me. I have another plan that I think will make you a better church planter." I took a napkin and sketched it out. "Stay at FSU, which is a great mission field. Train hard academically. Train hard in campus ministry." I charted out training events that would develop his skills. I emphasized developing deep spiritual disciplines.

"Do this, Roger, then go to seminary and you'll be a better church planter." But deep down, I wondered, "Lord, how is he going to preach without a full voice?"

Next week, Roger came back with the napkin. "OK, I'm going to do it." And for the next three years he did it.

Roger committed himself to regular quiet times—studying Scripture and a lot of prayer. He went to the Urbana missions conventions his freshman and senior years. He went overseas on a global project in Latin America. He served the fellowship as the Bible-study coordinator and president. He preached open air when Cliffe Knechtle, InterVarsity's open-air evangelist, came to town. People snickered at him, but Roger didn't care. He was living out the napkin. He became a communications major. He shared Jesus one-on-one in his scholarship house and with his classmates. Roger embraced the FSU campus and loved it as his mission field.

When we would meet, he would talk about how many churches he could start overseas and work himself out of a job. "Just think, Paul, if I can serve forty years, and they say it takes six years to start a church, I can plant seven churches in my lifetime!" I met with Roger regularly for four years. Every once in a while I'd ask, "How's the plan, Roger?" "On target. I'm following the napkin," he'd respond.

Roger graduated, became a deacon at a local church, married a wonderful woman, then entered Columbia Biblical Seminary in South Carolina. His fellow seminary students urged him to go into something else. They'd tell him, "Roger, you can't preach with your voice." He'd simply tell them, "Look, all I know is God called me to do this. I'm just being obedient."

During his last year at seminary, I visited Roger. "How's the plan?" "Still following the napkin," Roger said, but then he told me of a new development. He had just gone before the local presbytery to be licensed as a ministerial candidate. As he shared his testimony, a man walked into the back of the room. After listening to Roger for a few minutes, he leaned over and whispered to the chairman, "I can fix it."

He was an ear/nose/throat specialist. He had just spent several days at Harvard Medical School as part of a select group of American specialists chosen to meet with a Japanese physician who had discovered a way to give full speech back to people like Roger. The doctor took Roger on as his guinea pig, at no cost.

A few months later, my phone rang at home. "Hi Paul, this is Roger." "Roger who?" I couldn't place the voice. Then it hit me. His voice was deep. Roger would be able to preach the gospel.

In these last twenty years of knowing Roger, C. S. Lewis's words have come true. God's straight line has been drawn by Roger's life of gratitude and obedience to his Lord.

What's written on the napkin of your life? Do you have a napkin—in the deep recesses of your heart—that has your plan, your dreams, for your life? Will you hand it over to the Lord and ask him for his napkin for your life?

Oswald Chambers wrote, "One individual life may be of priceless value to God's purposes and yours may be that life."

Lou Whitaker put it this way: "If you're not living on the edge, you're taking up too much space."

Living Your Faith

1. Think about the statement "Slow down. Do less. Do better." As you seek to be a disciple of Jesus, in what areas do you need to slow down? Do less? Do better?

2. Are there failures in your life that keep you from growing in your walk with God? Do you believe God has forgiven you for them? What else do you need to move on?

3. If you don't already have one, who might be a good mentor or discipler for you? Is there anything keeping you from asking him or her soon?

Recommended Reading

Following Jesus in the "Real World" by Richard Lamb, InterVarsity Press.
A Long Obedience in the Same Direction by Eugene Peterson, InterVarsity Press.
Run with the Horses by Eugene Peterson, InterVarsity Press.